SIX YEARS IN THE
MALAY JUNGLE

An unposed photograph of Semang taken from conceal-
ment in the Pahang jungle. These Negritos were under
four feet six in height. A unique picture.

SIX YEARS IN THE MALAY JUNGLE

BY

CARVETH WELLS

Fellow of the Royal Geographical Society
Associate Member Institution of Civil Engineers

WITH A PREFACE BY

DR. FREDERIC AUGUSTUS LUCAS

Director Emeritus of the American
Museum of Natural History

ILLUSTRATIONS FROM PHOTOGRAPHS

SINGAPORE
OXFORD UNIVERSITY PRESS
OXFORD NEW YORK
1988

Oxford University Press

Oxford New York Toronto
Petaling Jaya Singapore Hong Kong Tokyo
Delhi Bombay Calcutta Madras Karachi
Nairobi Dar es Salaam Cape Town
Melbourne Auckland

and associates in
Beirut Berlin Ibadan Nicosia

OXFORD is a trademark of Oxford University Press

First published by Doubleday Publishing Company,
New York 1925
First issued as an Oxford University Press paperback 1988
This edition published in arrangement with
William Heinemann Limited

ISBN 0 19 588873 1

Printed in Malaysia by Peter Chong Printers Sdn. Bhd.
Published by Oxford University Press Pte. Ltd.,
Unit 221, Ubi Avenue 4, Singapore 1440

PREFACE

THE Malay Jungle is an interesting place—to read about—but to be sent there for two years and to be forced to stay there for six would try the temper and the constitution of most people.

And that was what happened to Mr. Wells—sent there in 1913 to survey a route for a railway, he was by the fortunes of war kept there for six years, for like the eruptions of Krakatau the effects of the World War were felt around the globe, especially in British Possessions.

Fortunately for Mr. Wells he possessed a stock of good nature, or philosophy, call it whichever you like, together with good powers of observation, and some of the things he saw and some of the things that happened he has told us in this book. Mr. Wells seems to take delight in so telling the truth that with Hamlet the reader will "doubt truth to be a liar," though naturally this is not so evident in his writing as in his lectures.

In my boyhood days, more than half a century ago, there was a story current among sailor men—quoted and misquoted often—of the Glasgow laddie who ran away to sea and after an absence of three years returned to visit his old grandmother, who naturally wished to hear of some of the wonderful things Jamie had seen. He told her of the Mountains of Sugar and Rivers of Rum he had seen in Jamaica, but this was only what the old lady expected. Then he related how, when they hove up anchor in the Red Sea, they brought up a wheel of one of Pharaoh's chariots—which did not surprise his aunt at all as the good book told how Pharaoh's host had been overwhelmed. But when, his imagination having given out, Jamie said that he had seen fishes that flew, the grandmother broke in: "Na, na, Jamie, ye must na tell lees to your old grannie."

So when Mr. Wells tells you of shooting a deer, which he put in his pocket and ate for supper, the reader—like the Chautauqua lady—is tempted to ask if Mr. Wells ever heard of Ananias. Yet Mr. Wells might have eaten two or three of these same little Chevrotains and still have gone to bed hungry.

And for the fish stories, the fish that climbed trees and winked at him, his floating islands—not in any sense deserts; and his other wonders of the East—they are no more imagination than Jamie's fish that flew. There are plenty of facts for the serious-minded in Mr. Wells's book, and for the very serious there is an appendix, compiled from official sources, on the Malay Peninsula and its resources.

This is not at all the preface I should have liked to write, but really Mr. Wells should have written his own introduction as it is difficult for anyone who has heard Mr. Wells lecture to do it justice.

F. A. LUCAS.

American Museum of Natural History
New York, Feb. 5, 1925

LIST OF ILLUSTRATIONS

INTRODUCTION

IT IS six years since I left the Malay jungle and came to America. At that time I had no more idea of writing a book than I had of lecturing. I came to regain my health and practice engineering.

No one is more conscious than I of the fact that there are many men far better qualified than I to write a book on the jungle of Malaya. In fact, I tremble at the thought of this book falling into the hands of such great authorities upon the country as Sir Hugh Clifford, Sir Frank Swettenham, and Sir George Maxwell.

"Six Years in the Malay Jungle," is, of course, very much condensed, from my notebooks, but I submit it as an absolutely true narrative of my personal experiences. It contains neither nature faking nor travellers' tales, although some people think I have an unusual way of making the truth sound like a lie. It is quite unintentional.

I have tried to be accurate in my natural history without being too technical, and where explanations of phenomena are given, they are my own and seem to me as good as those given by men who possess what I do not—a scientific background.

Although many of the names in the book are fictitious, the people really exist.

The reader must not think that the jungle life I have described is in any way typical of life in such cities as Singapore, Penang, and Kuala Lumpur. I can think of no more fascinating place for the tourist than the Malay Peninsula, for a short visit, and travellers around the world should never fail to go by train from Singapore to Penang, instead of remaining on the steamer. They will find excellent hotel service and as up-to-date railroad accommodation as in America or Europe.

If, however, you want to experience the real joy of jungle life, just try cutting your way clear across the native state of Pahang, in any direction you like, or make a little trip across the Serdang swamp in Kedah. Keep out of reach of railroads, roads, rest houses, and cold-storage food, and you will soon appreciate some of the descriptions in this book.

I am very grateful to Mr. Louis Froelick, editor of the *Asia* magazine, to Mr. William Beebe, and to the numerous members of the staff of the American Museum of Natural History, for the great assistance they have given me in answering so patiently my numerous questions.

I am very much indebted to Sir Edward Brockman and the Federated Malay States Bureau of

London for their kindness in permitting me to use government photographs and in supplying statistical information.

CARVETH WELLS.

Lapland,
   June, 1924.

SIX YEARS IN THE MALAY JUNGLE

CHAPTER I

ONE morning in May, after getting out of bed on the wrong side and making the baby cry, I determined to quit my job of Assistant Professor of Civil Engineering and look for something dangerous. With that in view I went up to London to present myself at the office of the Crown Agents for the Colonies and suggest that they needed a railroad engineer with American experience. Thinking that perhaps a little "pull" might be of assistance, I called upon Lord Halsbury, England's Lord Chancellor, at 9 o'clock one morning.

As I was ushered into the dining room I felt a strange sinking sensation when I realized that the only connection there was between me and the Lord Chancellor of Great Britain was the fact that I used to buy apples from his brother's little greengrocery store in Torquay, Devonshire, when I was a boy at school. Just as I was about to sneak out of the room, Lord Halsbury entered—a short, thick-set little man with rosy cheeks, over eighty, but erect and immaculately dressed. I had secured the introduction to the noble lord through my sister-in-law.

He said:

"Well, young man, what can I do for you?"

Swallowing my Adam's apple I said:

"I'm afraid you will think it awful cheek! But I wondered if you would recommend me to the Crown Agents for a job?"

He replied:

"Why, I'm very sorry, but I'm afraid I don't know you."

I said:

"Oh! but I knew your brother in Torquay. You know I used to buy apples from him!"

Lord Halsbury's manner immediately changed.

"I shall be delighted," he said, "to write to the Crown Agents and state the fact that you know my brother and that I know you to be a young man of remarkable initiative!"

I thanked him profusely and withdrew. A few days afterward I received instructions to call upon the Government's consulting engineers in Westminster, Messrs. Gregory, Eyles & Waring. My interview with Mr. Waring I shall never forget. He was at that time a very old man but was still responsible for practically all the appointments made by the Crown Agents. A noted civil engineer, he loved to talk about his jungle exploits, and instructed me in such matters as the art of walking across a slippery coconut log and a bamboo bridge, and as seasoning to his counsel added:

"We send dozens of young fellows like you abroad, and the Governments are continually asking for more. You see, they don't last long!"

At the end of the interview he said, "You are appointed a surveyor, and will sail for the Malay Peninsula within two weeks. Take my advice, keep your head cool and your stomach warm. Good-day."

And in two weeks from that date I was on my way to the jungle!

Those two weeks before sailing were spent in buying an outfit for life or death in the tropics. I spent nearly five hundred dollars in equipment that turned out to be absurdly useless except for the following articles, which were invaluable:

A waterproof canvas dunnage bag
A hair pillow with waterproof canvas cover
Mosquito boots and a fine mosquito net
A small airtight, watertight, tin trunk with a wooden bottom
A folding camp stool
A looking-glass in a wooden case
A medicine chest and medical book

The most useful medicines I carried were:

Quinine (the chloride, not the sulphate)
Aspirin

Chlorodyne	Zinc ointment
Eno's Fruit Salt	Vaseline
Sulphur ointment	Adhesive tape
Boracic lint	Castor oil
Permanganate of potash	Toothache drops
Iodoform	Seidlitz powders
Iodine	Plenty of bandages of lint

All of the so-called tropical clothes, underwear, cholera belts, the enormous pith helmet, and patent explorer's appliances too numerous to mention, were discarded when I reached Malay.   They might have been useful for a gentleman explorer of unlimited means and nothing to do except play at exploring; but for the practical engineer and jungle surveyor such things were impediments.   I bitterly regretted the expenditure of so much money uselessly when I needed it so badly, but I believe the same mistake is made over and over again by men going to the tropics for the first time.   It is nearly always best to wait until you arrive and then get a man to advise you as to the local customs and requirements.

One of the last persons I met before I sailed was a famous naturalist, Professor Albert Günther.   He was one of the members of the Challenger Expedition and had married my cousin.   I always loved to visit his house in Kew where he spent his time surrounded by books, animals, and elderly survivors of the Challenger Expedition.   He was probably greatest as an authority on fishes but he was also a wonderful all-round naturalist. It was he who first told me of the wonders of the Malay Peninsula. He advised me to spend all my spare time studying the unusual plant and animal life of the marvellous country to which I was going, and as I left him he said, "Plant citronella grass around your house and it will keep away the mosquitoes."

I took his advice and planted that luxuriant grass not only around many government houses but also for several miles on both sides of the railway embankment.

CHAPTER II

IT WAS not until the whistle blew and the R. M. S. *Simla* of the Peninsula and Oriental Line had cast off that I realized what I had done, and as I watched my wife waving to me and gradually fading away in the distance, I experienced the feeling of being tragic. But I comforted myself by saying, "What, after all, is two years' separation?"—little dreaming that long before two years would have elapsed there would be a World War and that the German cruiser *Emden* would be chasing my wife across the Indian Ocean. At the time I sailed, Lord Roberts was imploring England to prepare for war with Germany, but he was laughed at.

I did not take much interest in anything until we has passed Gibraltar and arrived at that wonderful little place, Malta. Malta is an island of stone in the Mediterranean, inhabited by a race of people who still speak the language of the Phœnicians. As the steamer entered the harbour it was surrounded by quaint-looking Maltese boats which are unlike those in any other part of the world. The island is very much like a huge gray fortress in appearance, with very little green apparent, set in a sea of brilliant blue. It was dreadfully hot when I landed and I was astonished to notice that the Maltese, both men and women, were dressed in black clothes. The women wear a strange headdress called a faldetta, or cloak of shame, to remind them of their dreadful sufferings at the hands of the early crusaders.

Nearly three years previously I had been in charge of a Maltese village at the White City, London's Coney Island, and there I had made friends with a Maltese girl called Virginia Camenzuli, an expert lace-maker. As soon as I landed in Malta, I visited the lace-making school on the Strada Mezzodi, and there, sitting at a table, just as I remembered her in London, was Virginia Camenzuli. Her astonishment at seeing me can be imagined. She left her work, and within an hour we had rounded up all the Maltese, both men and women, of whom I had had charge at the White City, and under their guidance I visited the principal sights on the island. Eventually I entered a strange little pony carriage and told the driver to take me to the steamer. I had no idea that Malta possessed several harbours, and when we arrived at the harbour there was no sign of my steamer. The driver suggested that I should try another harbour, and as I had only twenty minutes before the steamer was due to sail we started off at a gallop, driving madly through the crowded streets, scattering men and women and children and chickens in every direction, finally arriving at the correct harbour just as the steamer was heaving up her anchor. As I waved good-bye to my friends Virginia shouted, "Mind you go and see my brother. He is a policeman at Port Said."

Although the voyage through the Mediterranean was very calm and hot I saw no sign of the celebrated St. Elmo's Fire, and I was not at all sorry when the buildings of the Suez Canal Company Offices came into sight as we entered Port Said. Here the dazzling whiteness of everything made it difficult for me to open my eyes. In fact, all of us immediately purchased dark sun glasses.

I was very soon surrounded by a chattering group of guides who were eager to show me something wonderful. In every case what the guide had to show had to be whispered. I think that Port Said, if it is not now, certainly was the most immoral town I ever visited.

At that time both Cairo and Port Said were being drained for the first time in their history and there were immense piles of iron pipes, large enough to drive an automobile through, to be seen everywhere. Now the sewage from Cairo is pumped out on to the desert, after purification, and is returned to Cairo in the form of fresh vegetables.

Going through the Suez Canal is a fascinating experience. It is so narrow that on one occasion when we were anchored to enable a steamer to pass us in the opposite direction we actually shook hands with the passengers on the other ship. Every now and then we saw an Arab caravan crossing the desert, and once, on the Arabian side of the desert, a magnificent mirage. When it was dark searchlights were lit at the top of the masts and the course of the Canal could be traced for several miles ahead.

At the other end of the Canal is the town of Suez which is situated at the most northern extremity of the Red Sea. As we sailed along the coast of the Sinai Peninsula every one was straining to get a glimpse of Mt. Sinai, but we were not rewarded. At the end of the Red Sea is the Strait of Babelmandeb, and after passing through the Strait we anchored off the town of Aden at about seven o'clock in the evening. There was a strong breeze blowing, but the air was hot and full of fine sand. As soon as the boat anchored great lighters full of coal came alongside and the vessel was coaled by most frightful-looking specimens of humanity. Some were yellow and some were black and they all looked as if they either had or were just going to have cholera, which was then raging on shore. The 2,000 mile journey from Aden to Colombo across the Arabian Sea was a miserable experience. The monsoon was blowing in the direction of India and immense waves followed the ship all the way. Sometimes she would roll until the deck railing was awash. The ships that we passed fighting their way in the teeth of the monsoon were perfectly white, covered with salt from the top of the mast to the water line.

It is easy to tell when you have arrived at Ceylon because, when the boat is a considerable distance from the shore, an immense "LIPTON'S TEA" can be seen. No sooner had the steamer anchored at Colombo than a little boat put out from the shore. In it was seated a Cingalese. I couldn't tell what sex the person was because the men look like women. They wear skirts, have long hair which they do up in a knot at the back of their heads with a tortoise-shell comb that almost encircles the head, and they usually carry umbrellas. The Cingalese climbed up the companion-way and coming up to me said, "Do you want to buy some moonstones?" When I intimated that I wasn't in the least interested he seemed offended and proceeded to tell me of the various crowned heads to whom he had sold moonstones, ending by saying that he had sold moonstones to every officer of importance in the British Navy. Now this interested me because my wife's uncle was in the navy. It is true he had been retired for about twenty years, but I said to the Cingalese, "If you can convince me you sold my wife's uncle a moonstone, I will buy one." He said, "What was his name?" I replied, "Frederick Stirling." "Why, of course I sold him a moonstone," he said without hesitation. I said, "Prove it." He beckoned me to his boat and invited me on shore. Together we proceeded to his little jewellery store and in less time than it takes to tell it he produced from a cabinet a visiting card, yellow with age, on which was printed "Mr. Frederick Stirling, R. N."! It was the uncle's visiting card, and I had to buy a moonstone!

It is not generally known that Ceylon is still one of the greatest big game preserves in the world. In fact, Mr. William Beebe told me that some of his most thrilling experiences had been with wild animals in the forests here.

The journey of about a thousand miles from Colombo to Penang was the most delightful part of the whole voyage. No land was seen until Kedah Peak, one of the highest mountains in the Malay Peninsula, came into view. When we were more than ten miles from Penang the smell of the sea was distinctly mixed with the smell of spices. Flying fish were common.

Although the greatest authorities state that they move their wings I was unable to detect the slightest motion through field glasses. The movement must be extremely rapid. Several times on the voyage between Ceylon and Penang, flying fish a foot long landed on the deck of the steamer. I had one cooked for my breakfast one morning. It was delicious.

CHAPTER III

NEARLY five weeks after leaving London we sighted the Malay Peninsula. We had arrived in a part of the world that Darwin called "Topsy Turvy Land."

For instance, it is a place where there are no seasons to speak of, neither winter nor summer; no wet or dry season, and the sun rises and sets at practically the same time all the year round. The mean shade temperature at sea level (about eighty degrees) has not varied more than about three degrees for a hundred years, while out in the sun the temperature goes up to 154 or 160 on a warm day. Rain falls about two hundred and seventy days in the year but there is scarcely ever a wet day. The weather may be perfectly fine all the morning, then rain nine inches between noon and three o'clock, and be fine again for the evening. Throughout the whole time I was in the Peninsula I never knew rain to prevent survey work for a whole day.

I know of houses in Singapore where boats can be seen moored to the front door, but there is no water in sight. However, when it rains, the housekeeper goes shopping down a drain.

Alfred Russel Wallace said of Malay:

"No part of the world can offer a greater number of interesting facts for our contemplation, or furnish us with more extensive and varied materials for speculation in almost every great department of human knowledge."

I hesitate to set down the things I know to be true.

One evening in camp some of my Malay coolies asked me to tell them something about the country from which I had come, and as I had been on the survey of the Grand Trunk Pacific Railway in Canada, I thought that they might like to hear something about the American climate and told them that once I had seen ice come out of the sky in lumps big enough to break the windows in houses.

They looked at me and exclaimed, "*Bohong* [liar]!" You would be surprised if you knew how many white people say exactly the same thing after they hear me talk. In fact, I was once asked to deliver a lecture on the Malay Peninsula at a very intellectual place called Chautauqua Lake, in New York State, and at the conclusion of the lecture, when I offered to answer questions, a lady jumped up and called out before about six thousand people:

"Mr. Wells, have you ever heard of Ananias?"

The only explanation I can give for the strange things that are to be seen in the Malay Peninsula is that Nature seems to have been completely upset by the absence of any marked seasons.

You will find birds nesting in one tree and the same kind of bird moulting in another.

You may have a tree in your garden with fruit upon it, while your next-door neighbour has the same kind of tree just blossoming.

One of the Malay birds, a small parrakeet called the serindit, actually sleeps upside down! Another bird, called the bustard quail, is peculiar because the female is larger than the male; she lays the eggs but he sits on them, and during the mating season the females do the fighting for the males—everything is wrong!

Some of the old naturalists used to speculate as to whether Malay bees made honey, when there was no need of a winter store of food since there is no winter. Strangely enough they do make honey but they do not eat it. They live on nectar with the result that their honeycombs get bigger and bigger until they are sometimes hanging six feet long from the branch of some tall tree. After a while these huge honeycombs become so heavy that they fall down and at the base of some of the large jungle trees there are beeswax mines where people go to dig up beeswax.

The Malays are as anxious as we are to collect honeycomb, and if they see a big comb hanging on a tree, they make a lot of hardwood pegs and hammer them into the trees, one above the other, so as to make a kind of step ladder all the way up. When they have climbed to the honeycomb they light a bunch of grass, smoke away the bees and cut the honeycomb off. Frequently it crashes to the ground and they lose all the honey, which is not such a great calamity to the Malays because they don't eat the honey very much. They eat the young bees!

The Malays are Mongolians, and vary in colour from nearly white to the colour of chocolate. Their hair is usually black and straight and the girls often have quite nice complexions, a kind of a mixture between a peach and a cup of coffee. A girl thinks she is perfectly lovely if she has a yellow face. Both the men and the women wear skirts called "sarongs." The word "sarong" means an envelope in the Malay language, so they dress in envelopes. They don't use buttons, hooks, eyes, or strings and yet their clothes don't come off as easily as you would think. It takes them only a few seconds to dress and best of all, they dress and undress without undressing!

Malay parents never punish their children and the children always seem to be happy and contented. They eat when they like, sleep when they like, and go to school when they like. The girls marry when they are about twelve and the boys when they are about

Sakai belles. Malayan aboriginals are divided into two classes: Sakai and Semang. Many of the Sakai are quite attractive, except in their habits.

fourteen. Once I saw a little Malay boy running about with a long stick chasing a big dragon fly! I thought he was crazy but he managed to touch the fly with the end of the stick and catch it. The stick was covered with sticky stuff like a fly paper. He pulled the wings off the big fly and popped it into a box with a lot more; that night he went home and fried them in oil and served them for his dinner smothered with onions and shrimps!

It is not only the Malay Peninsula that is topsy-turvy, but the whole of the Malay Archipelago, including the Philippines. Take Java, for instance. If you go into the Javanese jungle you will find that the earthworms sing; they come out of the ground and whistle at you! Not so very far away are the Cocos Islands where the crabs eat the coconuts and the fish eat the coral, rats live on the tops of tall trees, and wells have both fresh and salt water in them.

But to return. The whole of the Malay Peninsula is situated within the North Equatorial zone, which extends ten degrees north of the Equator, and while the geographical Equator misses the Peninsula by about half a degree, yet the "Heat Equator" passes exactly through the middle of the country.

From Singapore to the most northerly part of the Peninsula is about seven hundred miles, and at its widest part it is two hundred and fifty miles wide while at its narrowest it is only about forty.

The area of the country is about 70,000 square miles and it may best be described as one vast jungle.

Even though it is the most important country in the world for the production of tin and rubber, only an insignificant fraction of the total jungle area has been cleared.

One convenient peculiarity about the Peninsula is that the magnetic compass points due north, thus simplifying surveying a good deal.

The Malays and even the aboriginals have their homes on the banks of rivers or on the sea coast, so that, strange as it may seem, the bulk of the Malay Peninsula has never been trodden by the foot of man.

It is still the home of tigers, black panthers, elephants, rhinoceroses, tapirs, snakes thirty feet long, insects over a foot long, butterflies and moths just about a foot wide, five different kinds of flying animals, forty different kinds of monkeys, and about twenty thousand wild women. (They are quite interesting.)

As you approach Penang, if you happen to be looking over the side of the ship, you can see snakes—red and yellow banded ones, big eight-foot fellows and frightfully poisonous—sporting in the water.

If you are lucky you may see a huge sea-eagle come

out of the sky, dive down, catch a snake, and carry him off into the air tearing him to pieces.

Even ten miles from the shore you may catch crocodiles twenty or even thirty feet long. Then as you get close to land, if you happen to be arriving at high tide you will be greeted with the smell of spices, but if you arrive at low tide you will be greeted with sulphuretted hydrogen and the smell of rotten eggs. You immediately ask where the smell comes from and a sailor will point out to you great mud flats that are exposed at low tide and from which is bubbling this evil-smelling gas, and there, crawling all over the mud, are fish, which climb up the trees and look at you.

Once I spent an hour watching one of these fish. I saw it come out of a hole in the ground, hop, skip, jump, and walk up to a tree, climb up, and deliberately wink its eye at me! Doctor Lucas told me that once he had the same experience, except that in his case the fish was in captivity, and that he thought that it winked its eye because it was dry. The fish I saw seemed to feel the heat, because after it had enjoyed the ozone, it climbed down, walked leisurely over to a pool, stood on the edge, dipped up some water in its fin and threw it over its head. I thought to myself, "If it should slip and fall in, it might be drowned." As a matter of fact, I was looking at the famous *periopthalmus schlosserii*, or Funny Fish!

CHAPTER IV

PENANG is really the name of an island, and the city itself is marked on the maps as Georgetown, but I seldom heard the latter name used in Malaya. The Chinese call Penang, Tanjong, meaning a point. The harbour is a fascinating place, full of strange-looking vessels, funny little Chinese steamers, Chinese junks, and sampans. All the native boats have a large pair of eyes painted on the bow without which the sailor would not consider the vessel seaworthy. The large liners tie up alongside the street just as they do in Bermuda, and the water front at Penang is as busy as an ant-hill day and night.

No sooner did I step on shore than a crowd of natives rushed up, snatched my baggage, and escorted me to a chattering mob of Chinese rickshaw coolies, all shouting at the same time: "*Tûan, tûan, ambil saya punya! Jangan ambil dia punya: buso punya!*" which means "Sir, sir, hire mine! Don't take his: it's a rotten one." Finally I picked out a nice rickshaw and beckoned to the men to place my baggage in another; but they promptly placed each piece of baggage in a separate carriage, and by the time I reached my hotel I had about nine carriages all in a line.

To say that I was hot but poorly describes my feelings. My thin summer suit felt like a blanket, and with the perspiration pouring off my chin I asked the proprietor of the hotel for a room with a bath.

"All the rooms have baths, sir," he replied.

Off I went, undressed, entered the bathroom, and then spent about ten minutes trying to find the bath. Finally I observed a large earthenware jar about four feet high, and perched up on a little shelf was a little tin cup! A friend of mine in the next room was evidently in the same fix except that he had managed to get into the jar and was vainly endeavouring to get out again. Instinct, however, told me how to take a bath in Malaya, namely, by standing outside the jar, dipping out the water with the little cup and pouring it over my head. This method of bathing is universal and wise, because to lie in a cold bath might produce a chill followed by death in the morning and burial in the afternoon. Things happen quickly in Malaya.

While I was daintily pouring the water over my head I heard a little pitter-patter and noticed two large frogs, followed by five smaller ones, hopping out from behind the jar and deliberately taking a bath with me. When I went out of the bathroom the frogs retired behind the jar, and every time I had a bath the same seven frogs joined me, and we became quite friendly.

Dinner that night was a splendid function, and it was hard to believe I was in the land of pirates and peacocks. Before entering the dining room I joined the gay crowd of people sitting at little round tables on the lawn of the Eastern and Oriental Hotel, drinking *pahits*, virgins, and other marvellous concoctions that invariably precede a meal in Malaya. A *pahit* is made as follows: two drops of Angostura Bitters are slowly rotated in a wineglass, which is then filled with either gin or whisky and slowly absorbed. A virgin is a similar mixture of vermouth and gin.

Dinner was served by numerous Chinese waiters to the music of a delightful orchestra conducted by a well-known Penang resident named Anthony.

In the dining room I saw a lot of little round tables all over the place, with Chinese waiters running about everywhere, and I sat down before the most delightful dinner. Just as I was beginning to eat my soup, I heard a noise like a smack, and there right in front of my plate I saw a lizard about four inches long. He scurried over the tablecloth, jumped to the floor, climbed up the wall, and ran across the ceiling. When I looked up, I saw about twenty or thirty lizards running about—upside down. Suddenly two of the lizards got hold of the same moth, and then they began to struggle, forgot themselves, let go and came right down into the middle of the soup plate.

The next time one of those lizards fell down I covered him with my handkerchief. As soon as he had stopped wriggling about underneath it, I picked it up and all that was left of the lizard was the tail. That kind of lizard, if you chase him, always breaks his tail off and, while you watch the tail run about, he gets away. But this is not all. Within about three weeks the lizard has another tail, and sometimes several new tails, growing out of the same place.

A little while after the first excitement an insect came to the window of the dining room and deliberately looked in to see if another insect like itself was inside. If there had been, I found out later, it would not have come in, for fear of being received as a bridegroom and eaten by the bride! But there happened to be just a few moths on the ceiling; so the insect came in. First it sat on the tablecloth in front of me and looked me up and down, as much as to say, "You are a very funny-looking object yourself." Then it began to say its prayers. In fact, it was a praying mantis and had innumerable relatives in the Peninsula. As it came toward me, I called the waiter and asked, "Here, is that thing going to bite?" "No, sir," he replied; "pick it up and have a look at it." To my surprise, I found that I could handle it without its minding a bit. I opened out its arms and saw for what evil end it kept them so piously folded: it had a lot of sharp spikes stuck all the way along them. When I let it go, it flew to the ceiling, caught hold of a moth, hugged it tight in those serrated arms, and cut it to pieces. And the moth's wings and legs dropped off and went into my plate. Once more a strangely garnished dish! This insect has been made famous by Francis Xavier who visited the Malay Peninsula and in writing to the Pope concerning his experiences said, "Even the insects say their prayers in this land, and when I ordered one to sing the praises of God also, it sang a merry canticle."

Personally I have the greatest respect for the powers of observation shown by those famous old travellers like Marco Polo, who said that he had seen many unicorns in Sumatra and that they were passing ugly animals! He spoke truthfully because he undoubtedly was referring to the one-horned Malayan rhinoceros.

After dinner, the tables were cleared away and dancing began. I remember one gentleman particularly, whose name is famous in the Far East, handsome, with gray hair and a bald head, who made a wonderful impression when he waltzed perfectly several times around the room with a *stenger* on his

bald head. A *stenger* is a half whisky and soda.
He was one of the famous Sarkies brothers, proprie-
tors of a chain of hotels in the Orient, and usually
to be found either at Raffles Hotel in Singapore or
the Eastern and Oriental Hotel, Penang.

Later we sat out on the lawn in the dreamy moonlight and watched the waves splash against the sea
wall and send showers of phosphorescent spray into
the air.   Far out to sea we every now and then caught
sight of the sudden flare of a fisherman's torchlight.

It was beautifully cool at nine o'clock and I decided to take a joy ride in a rickshaw. I could not
speak Malay, so I just smiled at the rickshaw coolie.
He grinned back and in a few minutes we were bowling along at a tremendous pace. Gradually the
strange native noises of the night grew louder and the
street lights brighter until we had to proceed very
slowly along a street that literally swarmed with
hundreds of natives of all nationalities.   Every now
and then we could hear the crash of a Chinese gong
or the plaintive tones of a one-string violin.

Suddenly the rickshaw stopped and the coolie,
looking back at me, nodded toward a house. I
glanced at it and this is exactly what I saw: right
on the sidewalk, without any door or window, was
a gorgeously furnished European drawing room.
Seated at a grand piano was a rather pretty girl, and

two other girls were sitting at a table reading magazines. All were in full evening dress, and as my coolie stopped running, the girls looked up and two of them came toward me. I was so inexperienced in those days that I gave the coolie a kick in the back and off he started, regretfully leaving the girls scowling in my direction. Soon he stopped again, looked back at me, and nodded to another house. This place looked decidedly interesting, and being more experienced now, I was all eyes and neck. There was a large open window, fitted with vertical iron bars about six inches apart. Around the window were standing several men of various nationalities, sizing up the points of the six little Japanese girls who were sitting at a table facing the windows and playing cards. They were dressed in gorgeous kimonos and their faces were painted almost as gorgeously. Four of the girls were fairly attractive, one was hideous, with a long face like the ones in Japanese pictures of women, and one was very pretty. I afterward discovered that my Western ideas of beauty were exactly the opposite of Oriental, because the hideous girl was the most beautiful, the prettiest one the most ugly, and the fairly attractive ones were fairly ugly. These Japanese girls entertained one for twelve hours for two dollars and a half American money, and at the end of the time supplied their

European guests with bacon and eggs for nothing. Unlike the European girls, whose charge for entertainment was fifteen dollars without the bacon and eggs, these little Japs took no notice whatever of the men inspecting. I gave my coolie another kick in the back, and the next house he took me to was quite different from the others. This one looked like an ordinary Chinese house with an open door. Standing at the door were two young Chinese girls wearing black trousers and white coats, while inside the house were two very fat old Chinese ladies dressed entirely in black and seated one on each side of a kind of an altar upon which joss sticks were burning. By this time my coolie did not wait for a kick in the back but just glanced at me and dashed along to another house which contained two Malay girls, dressed in European clothes, and then to another where there were two Tamil women wearing very little of anything, and finally to a vile place in which there were four Portuguese girls dressed in white muslin dresses, very pretty, but looking strangely out of place in such filthy surroundings.

This time the coolie put the shafts of the rickshaw on the ground and facing me began a most extraordinary flow of Chinese bad language and signs that were so eloquent that I had no difficulty in understanding that he was saying:

"Well, I have taken you from the top to the bottom! What the devil *do* you want?"

As I had seen quite a lot for my first evening in the country, I said:

"Hotel."

As we were returning I noticed a frightful pandemonium coming from a large barn-like structure. As there was a ticket office outside, I stopped my coolie, and beckoning him to wait, paid a dollar and found myself inside a Chinese theatre. It was packed with Chinese and there was a large gallery full as well at the back of the theatre. Upon the stage were several actors in gorgeous costumes making strange noises and speaking exactly like Punch and Judy marionettes. On one side of the stage was a Chinese orchestra of eight men, and wandering about the stage, dressed in black trousers and a white cotton undershirt, was a scene-shifter, casually arranging scenery and taking no notice whatever of the actors or the audience. Every now and then, after the leading actor had evidently made a joke in Chinese, a man gave a huge gong a terrific whack, and this notified the audience that they were supposed to laugh.

What interested me far more than the play was the audience. Everyone was eating and all kinds of food and delicacies were offered for sale throughout the acting. Two attendants walked about continually with wet towels with which they wiped the faces of the audience, and I was horrified when I saw the towel coming my way. After the audience on the floor had had their faces wiped, the towels were flung dexterously up to the attendants in the gallery who commenced face-wiping up there. The most expensive seat in the theatre insures the first wipe, but of course the gallery patrons have the honour of using the same towel as their richer brethren below.

I arrived at the hotel about midnight, and as we passed through the still-crowded streets it was interesting to see what hundreds of natives there were who were sleeping in the doorways and on the pavements, homeless. The neighbourhood about the hotel was peaceful, and I long to hear once more the strange twittering of the swallows, the funny little "Chee-chuck," of the house lizards, and the peculiar "Conk Conk Conk" of the "Knocking-on-the-Ice-Bird" that is heard all through the tropical night.

As I went up to my bedroom one of the house boys asked me if I wanted a "Dutch Wife."

With vivid recollection of the rickshaw coolie who, in response to my innocent desire to be taken for a moonlight ride, had just driven me from one end to the other of Penang's cosmopolitan *Yoshiwara*, I looked at the boy with great interest as he went to a cupboard.

"*Tûan* will sleep better with a Dutch Wife," he said, and he produced a long hard bolster!

I accepted his kind offer and rolled into bed feeling foolish and wondering what on earth to do with the bolster. At the foot of the bed was a thick blanket, but as the temperature in the room was eight-two degrees I threw out the blanket and tried to sleep. Soon I was so hot that I kept sticking one of my legs and one arm up in the air to ventilate them and keep them dry. But they got so tired that with a flash I thought of my "Dutch Wife." It was a perfectly splendid idea, because all that was necessary was to place the long bolster in front, put one leg and one arm over it, and thus go to sleep with air freely circulating between my limbs. I slept beautifully until two o'clock in the morning, when the temperature in the bedroom dropped two degrees, from 82 to 80, and I was so cold that I recovered the blanket and was very glad to have it.

About four o'clock in the morning I was disturbed by a peculiar noise, and as I listened intently in the still night I realized that pigs were being slaughtered in various parts of the city. It was a most dreadful experience; first the terrified squeaks and grunts as the butcher caught the pig; then the prolonged squealing as the wretched pig was thrown down upon the block, then a ghastly bubbling squeal, and I knew that the knife had been thrust into his throat; and gradually the squeals became weaker and weaker until with a faint despairing cry they stopped. No sooner had silence come than the same unearthly shrieks filled the air as another pig was caught.

This happens at exactly the same time every morning in every town and village where there is any Chinese population.

The sun rises at about six o'clock all year round in Malaya. I was awakened at that hour by the loud buzzing of a big black boring bee, the carpenter bee, as it flew into the bedroom and disappeared into a hole in the ceiling. As I lay awake, lazily comfortable, I watched the insect at work. He would stay in his hole about a minute and then fly out of the window only to return again shortly and make straight for the same hole in the ceiling. I noticed that he always went to and from a large bush of scarlet hibiscus that was growing on the lawn of the hotel.

At seven o'clock a Chinese "boy" dressed in white entered the bedroom and placed beside me a tray containing tea, toast, and several mangosteens, the most delicious and refreshing fruit of Malaysia Most tropical fruits usually have a rather insipid taste and, although delicious, make one long for a good crisp apple or juicy Bartlett pear, but the mangosteen is different. It is about as large as a small orange, dark brown or violet in colour, with a thick, soft, and easily broken shell. There are often little lumps of a yellow substance either on the outside or the inside, and it was hard to realize that this was gamboge, used by artists as a water-colour paint.

Inside the shell are what look like the divisions of a small white orange. The number of the divisions varies considerably, from three to seven or even eight. This white part is very sweet, juicy, and of exquisite flavour. Many unsuccessful attempts were made to transport mangosteens to England in order that Queen Victoria might taste one. She is said to have tasted every fruit in the British Empire except a mangosteen and a durian.

A rich brown dye is extracted from the shell of the mangosteen and often used by ladies to dye their hair auburn.

When I had dressed I went out for a rickshaw ride before breakfast, through the same streets I had visited the night before, but the houses were closed and silent while outside them were Tamils selling baskets of lovely roses fresh with dew still sparkling on their petals. Roses do not, of course, grow down in the town of Penang, but there are large rose gardens high up on the hill behind the city.

The market-place was crowded with the Chinese

cooks from the various European houses and hotels, purchasing their daily supplies. Housekeeping for the white wife in Malaya is very different from house-keeping at home. The thrifty housewife is an utter failure in the Orient. In their eagerness to save money many newly married girls keep strict accounts and carefully ration the cook. In fact, some are foolish enough to try to do the cooking as well as the marketing themselves; but it never works and in-variably results in the despairing collapse of the well-meaning bride; for the servants all leave in con-tempt. An experienced wife manages her housekeeping very much like this: She has a daily interview with her Chinese cook and gives him a rough idea of the number of people she expects to meals that day. The cook asks for, say, two or three dollars and goes off to market. Upon his return he gives his mistress an account of the money, and there is rarely any change. A wise woman accepts the inevitable. The unwise doubts the cook's word, goes to market her-self and discovers that the cook's prices are much higher than those in the market. She then accuses the cook of cheating and he says, "All right, *mem* will go to market." (Mem is the Indian equivalent of madam.)

Mem goes the next day and finds that all the prices in the market have suddenly risen enormously. She is compelled to let the cook resume his marketing. As a matter of fact, since a Chinaman accepts a place as cook for perhaps fifteen dollars gold a month, he expects to make his profit out of the marketing, and it is wisest and cheapest to allow him this privilege.

The market-place of any Oriental town is fascinating. Here and there in Penang Market were Chinamen with elaborate portable restaurants. When the proprietor met a client, he would set the whole restaurant down, produce the menu, take the order, cook and serve it there and then. There were numerous peddlers who had different methods of drawing attention to their wares. Some were jingling little pieces of metal, another had a little drum to which was attached two little weights on a string, so that by rotating the drum rapidly the weights beat a merry tattoo. One old Chinaman was knocking two pieces of bamboo together, making a noise very much like castanets. Another was blowing a horn. Every housekeeper knew the meaning of every sound.

I saw one horrible sight! It was the pork butcher of the still night. He was selling only fat, and people were crowding around him buying large slabs of it.

In one corner of the market was a professional tooth extractor, not necessarily a dentist. As evidence of his skill he had a box containing thousands of teeth which his prospective clients were morbidly examining. The itinerant barber with his shop was an object lesson in compactness. He stopped in the street and in less than a minute had a basin, chair, and his client ready for business. He poured some water out of a bottle into the basin. He then not only shaved his customer but removed his eyebrows, cleaned his nose and ears, and finally scraped his tongue. The water was then poured back into the bottle for future use, and in a few moments he had packed up the barber's shop and moved along. Strangely enough I notice that our drug stores nowadays are selling tongue scrapers of exactly the same pattern as those the Chinese have used for ages.

I came to a large Chinese restaurant, the windows of which were full of dreadful dead ducks, all kinds of pork, and several pigs roasted whole and covered with brown, shining "crackling." Outside the shop was the fattest Chinaman I have ever seen. He was the proprietor of the pork and was dressed in two garments consisting of a pair of black baggy trousers, wrapped tightly around and over his hips but underneath his ponderous paunch, and a white cotton undershirt that was wrinkled up until it was only covering his chest and his shoulders. He was seated on a stool, groaning and regarding me with a doleful look, while he pressed against his stomach a mechanical vibrator, the handle of which he was slowly turning.

That market-place would have entertained me for days but I had to hurry back to breakfast and then down town to do some shopping. By 11 o'clock in the morning the streets and stores were crowded with Europeans, men and women, all dressed in white. The ladies invariably go down town in the morning before it is too hot and indulge in ice creams or gin slings, the latter being the most refreshing drink in the Orient. It is made with gin, cherry brandy, fresh limes, soda water, and sugar, all well mixed with a swizzle stick. I discovered a celebrated place, the Bodega, where every conceivable kind of drink was concocted for every conceivable kind of white man, from beachcombers to millionaires.

I received an invitation that day to a curry tiffin from a married couple who had spent years in Penang. This was my first real curry, and I could eat only about one tenth of the amount devoured by my friend and his wife, although I can now compete with any one. The curry was so hot that it burned my mouth, but I found that a mouthful of banana in between the curry soothed the burning. Besides the curry and the rice were served more than twenty different kinds of trimmings or *sambals:* chopped pineapple, prehistoric Chinese eggs, Chile paste, *blachan* (a putrid paste made of rotten shrimps and fish), cucumber, grated coconut, turtles' eggs, and chutney.

Copious draughts of beer washed down the curry which was followed by a dessert consisting of *gula malacca*, which is one of my favourite puddings. It consists of the largest kind of pearl tapioca, carefully boiled, strained, and set to cool, looking like a mass of frogs' eggs. Two sauces are then poured over the tapioca. The first is a syrup made of sugar from the coconut palm and looks like thin treacle; the second is a creamy white milk made as follows: a fresh coconut is grated and to it is added about half a pint of cold water. The coconut is then squeezed in the hands and the milky liquid strained off and served.

After luncheon the three of us retired, undressed, and slept in a bath of perspiration until half-past four. Then we all had a shower bath, dressed in clean white clothes, and proceeded to the club. As I rode to the club in a rickshaw I passed my friend, the fat restaurant-keeper, riding with his wife in a Rolls-Royce, looking quite happy and enjoying the sensation his wife was causing, she being gorgeously dressed and smothered in jewellery with diamonds in her ears as big as nickels.

A band was playing at the club and around the

bandstand were numerous native nursemaids, Indian, Chinese, and Malay, looking after a crowd of pretty white children, most of whom spoke English not half as well as Malay. Their mothers were in the club variously engaged. Some were playing bridge. They were smoking and had a *suku* beside them (a *suku* is a quarter whisky and soda). Others were having afternoon tea. Here and there in a confidential corner were couples, usually a very pretty woman and a very good-looking man, thoroughly enjoying each other's company, the best of good friends, and quite devoted—married, of course, but not to each other. Across the room in sight of them was another couple, equally happy, though married, but not to each other. It was not at all uncommon to find instances of "half-time change over," and the mutual switching over from one's own wife or husband to someone else's.

I wish I could have remained in Penang, but I was under agreement to survey a railroad through the jungle and the next day I started off for the mainland.

CHAPTER V

PENANG has a magnificent railroad station but no railroad. The actual railhead is on the mainland of the Peninsula at a little town called Prai. The journey from Penang to Prai was a delightful trip, which lasted about half an hour, in a palatial steam yacht painted white and gleaming with polished brass fittings. The sea was as smooth as glass and seemed literally to swarm with all sorts of life from sea-snakes to flying fish.

The Malays are great fishermen, and their elaborate fish traps look like small villages far out at sea, with miles of bamboo fences carefully constructed so as to guide the fish into the traps.

I once met an old fisherman whose arm was in a dreadful state of mortification, and he told me that while taking fish out of a trap he had been bitten on the finger by a sea-snake. His arm ought to have been amputated, because he was dying by inches, but he refused to enter a hospital. Very few Malays ever enter a European hospital, for they prefer to be ill in their own homes, and even lunatics and lepers are to be found in the native "kampongs." Lunatics are confined in stocks or tied up with a chain, or else they are perpetually confined in a sort of a kennel underneath the house.   Although the idea is purely fantastic, Malays firmly believe that if a patient is admitted to one of our hospitals, and is not immediately cured, the white doctor poisons him off! This is due to the fact that a very large percentage of patients die within twenty-four hours of admission.

Says the Malay to himself: "See how many go in and how few come out.   There must be a reason for this and the reason is that if a white doctor sees that he cannot cure a patient he is ashamed, and in order that the person shall not linger and bring shame upon the art and practice of medicine, he poisons him."

The real reason for the enormous number of deaths is that the Malays never take a man to the hospital until they have tried every other means of curing him, and when the unhappy patient is at his last gasp they take him off to the hospital.

As the boat approached the mainland I could see the great mangrove swamps that make the West Coast of the Peninsula so different from the beautiful sandy shores of the East Coast.   Suddenly we left the open sea and glided into the mouth of the Prai River.   The river looked deep and oily and its banks were not visible because of the dense mangrove trees growing in the water.   Except for the vibration of the vessel, there was absolute silence, broken once by a loud splash as a crocodile that had been sleeping on a mud-bank aroused and floundered into the water.

A crocodile is an interesting animal. No one that I have ever met knows how long or how old he grows. In fact, sacred crocodiles have been kept in captivity for more than a century and observed all the time, but the crocodiles never die—the observers do! Their teeth are renewed over and over again. The eyes, ears, and nostrils are all conveniently situated on top of the head so that the crocodile can float with his body almost completely submerged but still see, smell, and hear. When he dives he closes his eyes and looks through his eyelids!

The mouths of the Malay rivers are infested with crocodiles and it is fairly common to meet natives with only one hand, the other having provided a tasty *hors d'œuvre* for one of these reptiles.

Once while I was in Prai, the small town opposite Penang, I was standing on the veranda of a bungalow early one morning about sunrise when I saw an old Tamil running as hard as he could, yelling his head off, because he was followed closely by an enormous crocodile. This one was standing well up from the ground, running fast on all fours with his huge mouth snapping at the Tamil. As the strange couple passed the police station, a native policeman rushed out and shot the infuriated animal. The old Tamil explained that he had just entered the river for his morning dip when Mr. Croc snapped at him, missed his arm by inches, and in rage and disappointment chased him into the village. As is customary when a crocodile is killed, he was cut open and the contents of his stomach examined. In this case there were two pairs of women's bangles and several small stones! The Malays say that when a crocodile eats a person or enters a new river he swallows a stone, which is his method of keeping accounts. His usual method of attack is to sneak up to his victim and by a sudden swing of his powerful tail, knock him into the river. He does not tear you to pieces but drags you under the water, pokes you into the mud at the bottom of the river, and drowns you. He does not injure you in any other way. Then, according to the Malays, the crocodile rises to the surface of the water, looks up to heaven, and calls on God to witness that he is not drowning you—that the water is. This interesting piece of folklore corresponds to our own idea of crocodile tears. After about two weeks the crocodile returns, drags you out, and you promptly fall into pieces of convenient size to be swallowed. After his meal, he frequently crawls out of the water on to a mud-bank, opens his mouth, and waits until a little bird, sometimes called a Zic-Zac, enters his mouth and picks his teeth.

This sounds like a traveller's tale but we have known about it since the days of Herodotus. The reason for the bird's action is that a crocodile's mouth is usually infested with leeches and other parasites which the crocodile is only too delighted to give the bird.

A mother crocodile lays her eggs usually upon a river bank close to the water and carefully covers them with rubbish and leaves. Although she does not incubate the eggs herself, yet in some mysterious way she knows exactly when they will hatch, and then, according to the Malays, the old crocodile returns to the nest and watches the little ones as they appear. Some make straight for the river, others for the jungle. Those that head for the jungle are chased and eaten by the fond mother. A few, however, escape her attention and enter the jungle, where, according to the Malays, they eventually turn into tigers. Crocodiles are very fond of dogs.

As we passed up the river, no jungle was to be seen, but only those dreadful mangrove swamps that have seldom been penetrated by man. Hundreds of climbing fish were scampering about on the mud, enjoying the fresh air. Hundreds of fiddler crabs were waving frantically to their fiancées. These little flirts have been waving to their lady loves so incessantly that the hand with which they wave—it may be either the right or the left—has developed until it is about ten times as large as the hand they eat with! Since the demure little girl crabs never wave back to their lovers, their hands are quite normal in size. Within an hour of leaving Penang, we glided alongside the railway station at Prai and in a few minutes I was seated in a modern Pullman car. I was the only white passenger, but there were several wealthy Chinese in the car, faultlessly dressed in white duck with coat buttons made of English gold sovereigns, and one I noticed had buttons made of American five-dollar gold pieces. Except for the Pullman car, the rest of the train was packed with a chattering mob of natives of every conceivable nationality. Chinese and Chetties, Tamils and Turks, Sikhs, Afghans, and Arabs, all mixed up with Malays. Some were laughing, others quarrelling, and all of them were suffering from the intense heat.

Before the train started, the man who corresponds to our train news agent passed down the platform selling refreshments through the windows of the carriages. The most popular sellers were slices of pineapple carved into strange shapes, short lengths of sugar cane, and small seeds called *kachang*, which are eaten as peanuts are eaten in America.

The railroad was one meter in gauge, and the whole rail system was so elaborately interlocked that accidents were of very rare occurrence. The station master was a Jafna Tamil who talked *chi-chi* English. The ticket puncher, Ram Singh, was a Sikh, one of those Indians who never shave. He had wrapped his beard around his ears, and, of course, wore the iron bangle of his religion. Like most Sikhs he had very thin legs and was wearing puttees and enormous army boots. It was remarkable to observe how this man, from one of the proudest and bravest races in India, looked down upon the native passengers who, in their eagerness to catch the train, which wasn't going to start for at least half an hour, did not want to wait and have their tickets punched! But Ram Singh rammed them back, clutched one Chinaman by his pigtail, and controlled a mob of about sixty howling natives as if they were sheep.

As there were a few minutes to spare, I went into the refreshment room and was introduced to a celebrated drink called tonic. It is very much like slightly sweet soda water but flavoured with quinine. While I was sipping my tonic a white man came into the room carrying a large glass jar in which was a black cobra.

"Boy! *Bawa satu* bottle gin *lekas!* [Boy! Bring me a bottle of gin quick!]" he cried.

While I wondered what he was going to do with the gin he opened the bottle and began to pour it very carefully into the glass jar containing that deadly snake. As the reptile felt the liquid touching it, it began writhing madly and opening wide its frightful mouth. Suddenly I was horrified to see that it had managed to get its head out of the bottle, but the man, quickly grabbing a tablecloth, jammed the head back into the gin.

Soon the snake's struggles stopped, and as he watched its last movements, the man said:

"Lucky snake! To drown in gin."

And I immediately thought of that personage in English history who was drowned in a barrel of Malmsey wine!

On my way back to the train, as I passed Ram Singh, he clicked his heels and came smartly to the salute, and at last I realized that for the first time in my life I was a man of importance. Soon I noticed the station master walking along the platform carrying in his hand a round brass disc, about four inches in diameter, which he handed to the engine driver. This was the permission to start, and with a shrill toot upon the whistle we puffed out of Prai.

At the first station the engine driver gave the brass disc to the station master who took it to his office and placed it in an automatic machine, which delivered him a new disc. This new disc was handed to the engine driver and off we started again. It was a revelation to find in one of its remotest countries probably the most up-to-date railroad in the world, fitted with every conceivable safety device. The only trouble is that the Malays, who own the country, are not yet educated to the rights of a railroad. They think nothing of tying up a cow to one of the rails so that it may graze on the embankment, or of tearing down the expensive wire fence along the right of way so that they can use the wire for tying up their boats.

In the olden days steel was in great demand from traders, but nowadays, in Kelantan, for instance, when I was in charge of the railway there, the Malays occasionally removed a rail length during the night. It was never seen again and was probably converted immediately into knives and spearheads. This makes night rides in trains an exciting experience.

The first part of the journey was very picturesque, because it had been surveyed in the good old days by contract, when the contracting engineer was paid so much a mile for his work. Consequently, the longer the railway, the more money for the contractor, and the result was a regular scenic railway full of curves.

In one place the train ran along the base of some immense limestone cliffs, sparkling in the sun, and for miles the railroad was ballasted with white marble.

The Malay Peninsula is a mass of mountains intersected in every direction by rivers and small streams. Running down the middle of the Peninsula, but nearer the East than the West Coast, is a range of granite mountains. Generally speaking, the rivers on the East Coast are short and swift while those on the West Coast are much longer and more sluggish. The mountains are not high, the highest being only eight thousand feet, but they are covered with jungle and luxuriant vegetation. In many places the granite has weathered until it is so soft that it can be dug up with a spade. The valleys are full of the soil washed by torrential rains from the mountains, and underneath this, but on top of the disintegrated granite, there are those immense deposits of nearly pure tin which provide the world with more than half its supply.

For centuries the Chinese have been mining this metal by the open cast method, and have laid waste enormous areas of the country, leaving huge holes and heaps of tailings. Owing to their antiquated methods of mining, the Chinese recovered only a portion of the tin, and nowadays, in certain districts, huge mechanical dredges are systematically remin-

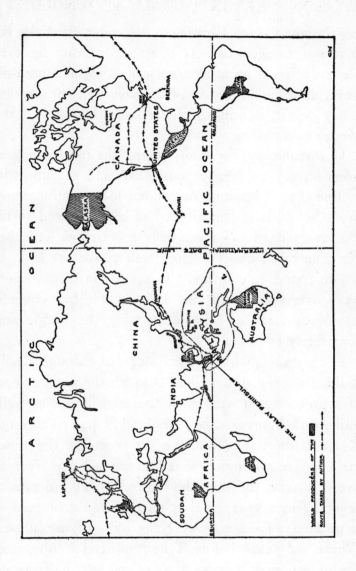

WORLD PRODUCERS OF THE
ROUTE TAKEN BY AUTHOR. ╍╍╍╍

ARCTIC OCEAN

PACIFIC OCEAN

ALASKA

CANADA

UNITED STATES

BERMUDA

HAWAII

INTERNATIONAL DATE LINE

CHINA

INDIA

ASIA

AUSTRALIA

THE MALAY PENINSULA

AFRICA

SOUDAN

LAPLAND

EQUATOR

YOKOHAMA

PHILIPPINE

GALAPAGOS

49

ing the abandoned Chinese mines, recovering the tin that was overlooked. It is an astonishing sight to see one of these great iron vessels, as big as a man-o'-war, full of machinery and men, slowly moving across a dry desert, floating in an artificial lake which the dredge takes along with it.

Unfortunately, for many years, the mining operations have been poorly controlled, and the fine silt, so fine that it remains suspended in water for many miles before it is deposited, has been allowed to fill the rivers until the river beds themselves have become elevated and are often well above the level of the surrounding country. In many places the rivers have overflowed and the fine red silt has covered enormous areas of land, destroying the jungle and completely covering towns.

For instance, when the train passed through Kuala Kubu I got out and walked through the main streets of a pretty town with good thoroughfares and well-built brick houses. Six years later, I passed through Kuala Kubu again, but the silt from the tin mines far away in the mountains had caused the river to overflow, and the town had silted up at the rate of several feet a year, so that all that could be seen of large areas of the city were the roofs of the houses. Where six years before I had noticed a fine steel bridge was now a great mass of red silt, halfway up the side of the steel girders.   Probably by this time the bridge will have been completely covered and the houses gone altogether.   The bridges on the railroad in this locality had to be raised several feet every year, and after a time the whole railway near the town was abandoned and rebuilt higher up the mountains.

My instructions were to report to the chief resident engineer of construction, Mr. Openshaw, at his office in Seremban, a large town in the state of Negri Sembilan.

Upon arrival of the train I was directed to a rather dilapidated wooden bungalow with a thatched roof. As I walked up the steps I noticed sitting in a row on a bench six stalwart Sikhs with guns and uniforms. They paid no attention to me until I was exactly opposite them, and then they all sprang to attention, presented arms, and saluted me with a clatter of muskets.

I almost fainted, but managed to walk past them, looking as important as I could after being almost frightened out of my life.   The next thing I saw was a little black Tamil boy sitting on a bench languidly jerking backward and forward a rope which was attached to his big toe and which disappeared through a hole in the wall.   I entered the room and presented my credentials to a smart little man who had the smallest hands and feet I had ever seen. He was dressed in white, and over his head was a punkah, slowly swinging, which was worked by the boy outside with the rope on his toe. After receiving me cordially, Mr. Openshaw told me to take my belongings to the Rest House and get myself an outfit for camp. Inwardly I thanked Heaven he couldn't see the marvellous outfit which I had purchased in London, and passed out of his presence. As I went by the six Sikhs they again sprang to arms, but I was prepared this time and gave them a military salute with the wrong hand, and came near falling down the steps of the bungalow in my embarrassment.

In a few moments I was walking through a lovely garden to the government Rest House. It was exactly midday, and I was interested to observe that my shadow had disappeared. The Rest House was crowded with Europeans, most of them planters from neighbouring rubber estates. There was much yelling of "boy" as a couple of busy Chinese boys rushed about dispensing drinks of various descriptions.

When I entered the dining room and had sat down I felt that someone was staring at me. I looked up and there in front of me was a man about thirty. His face seemed familiar, and exactly as he said, "Wells!" I said, "Aldrich!" It was sixteen years since we had been chums at St. Paul's School, London, and we had not met since that time.   Aldrich was in charge of a rubber estate.   He took me down to the native quarter of Seremban, to a Chinese tailor, who made me four suits of khaki clothes and two suits of white duck, beautifully finished and a perfect fit for less than two dollars a suit in American money.   That was ten years ago, and I still wear the clothes during the summer time here in America.   I also had six pairs of white canvas boots made to measure, at one dollar a pair.   The reason that canvas is used instead of leather is that water can get out of your boots just as easily as it gets in.   We went over the outfit I had brought with me, and after selecting the articles I have already enumerated, we packed up all the rest, clothes and everything, and left them behind at the Rest House.   I did not unpack them until six years afterward when I arrived in America, when, thanks to my airtight tin trunk, the clothes were as good as new.

The next night I arrived at a tiny place in the jungle, but still on the railroad, called Kuala Krau, and slept there in the railway Rest House.   Just as I was about to go to bed, in walked a man covered with mud and leeches, and once more I found myself face to face with an old schoolfellow, Hutton, who was the railroad engineer at the "end of steel" for which I was bound myself.

As we sat on the veranda that evening I had my first experience of life in the jungle. During the afternoon I had not noticed anything particularly unusual, simply the steady hum of the insects, just as we are accustomed to in the summer over here, but promptly at 6:30 P. M. a most extraordinary noise commenced. First of all, there was a loud *toot, toot, toot*, like blasts upon a child's tin trumpet, then an infernal buzzing shriek, then a perfect roar of countless frogs, followed by numerous other distinct and different sounds, until the noise was so deafening that speaking was difficult. It reminded me of Chicago, but it was only the noise of insects in the jungle waking up for the night or else saying good-night to one another, I never knew which; but promptly at 7 o'clock, as suddenly as they had begun, the noises ceased and it was dark. Occasionally I heard a cricket, or the sudden chatter of a monkey quarrelling with his bedfellow, or the far-distant call of a peacock.

That evening, much to the amusement and disdain of Hutton, who was barefoot, I put on my new mosquito boots. These boots are like ordinary high riding boots, but are made of soft leather with soft soles and are worn to protect the legs and ankles from the bite of the *Anopheles* mosquito. This is the malaria-carrying mosquito which almost invariably flies close to the ground. It can easily be recognized by the position it adopts when resting, because it stands on its head. I wore my mosquito boots after dark regularly for nearly a year, until they were worn out. Then I went barefoot like my companion and within three weeks had malarial fever.

The next morning Hutton and I boarded a construction train but later transferred to a trolley car, pushed by a couple of barefoot Indians who ran for hours in the blazing sun, balancing themselves on top of the steel rail while they kept us moving at about seven or eight miles an hour until we reached the end of the railway.

At the railhead a village called Tembeling had sprung up, close to the bank of the Jelei River, and while I was in that locality, Mr. William Beebe was there, looking for pheasants. We used the same coolies. He is the only man I ever heard of who actually has had a hand-to-hand encounter with a King cobra, the most dangerous snake in the world—but that is his story.

It was not long before a boat arrived at Tembeling to fetch me, and at 6 o'clock one morning, just as the sun was rising, I started through the jungle to the river Jelei.

CHAPTER VI

WE STARTED away in Indian file. That is to say, I had one man in front of me; then I came; then the coolies, carrying my baggage. We always walked like that, to look out for snakes. I had heard that in India twenty thousand people a year were killed by snakes; so I hired somebody to walk in front of me, and then, if any one got bitten, he was the man. Finally we reached a river and found two boats waiting for us. The Malays built sunshades over the boats and placed a mattress at the bottom of my boat, and off we went. I knew the superstitious nature of the Malay well enough not to be surprised when an old woman came up as I was leaving Tembeling and offered me a black cat. "Here's a cat for you," she said. I did not want the cat—it had a crooked tail. I did not know then that Malay cats always do have crooked tails and that it is quite natural for them to have unnatural tails.

"If you take the cat," said she, "you may come back again." I took the cat!

The boat was a very gracefully carved dugout, about twenty-five feet long and three feet wide. The

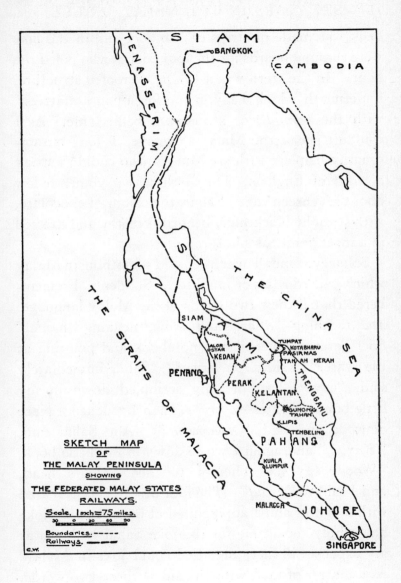

SKETCH MAP
OF
THE MALAY PENINSULA
SHOWING
THE FEDERATED MALAY STATES
RAILWAYS.

Scale. 1 inch = 75 miles.

Boundaries. -----
Railways. ━━━━

C.W.

deck was made of strips of bamboo, and in the bow were running boards for the four coolies who poled the boat.   In the stern was a *kajang*, or roofed structure, underneath which I lay in comfort upon a mattress, with the *kamudi*, or steersman, behind me.   As I couldn't speak the Malay language, I felt extraordinarily helpless with six Malays who couldn't speak a word of English.   The sixth was a young fellow about seventeen called Sahar, the colour of chocolate, with straight black hair, beautiful teeth, and dressed in a most gorgeous silk sarong.

Sahar eyed me all over, then said something in Malay which caused roars of laughter.   Suddenly, I remembered that I knew two words of the Malay language: *apa*, meaning "what," and *nama*, meaning "name." So I got out a pencil and notebook and pointing at the water I said, *Apa nama?*"   Sahar immediately said, "*Ayer.*"   I hurriedly scribbled down in my little book, "Water—*ayer.*"   Then I touched a piece of wood and said, "*Apa nama?*"   And Sahar said, "*Kayou,*" and again I wrote down in my little book, "Wood—*kayou.*"   Then I touched Sahar's head, and I said, "*Kayou!*"   The four other Malays roared with laughter and I appreciated at once that my joke had amply repaid me for the joke Sahar had had at my expense; in fact, already I could joke in Malay! As a matter of fact, with the aid of those two words, *apa nama*, I acquired an excellent vocabulary, and I discovered that by stringing the words together in the same order as English I could usually make myself understood. Of course, it took me several years to speak Malay even very poorly, but only a few hours to make myself understood.

At eleven o'clock that morning we landed on a sand-bank and the Malays began to cook rice. Each man had a small brass pot which he supported on three little wooden pegs driven into the sand. Two or three handfuls of rice were placed in the pot and barely covered with cold water. A fire was lighted, and as soon as the water began to boil, the fire was removed except for a few glowing embers. The rice was stirred several times at intervals and left with the cover on in between the stirrings. After about twenty minutes, it had completely absorbed all the water and was beautifully cooked, each grain separate. The Malays sat on their haunches and turned the rice out on to a large leaf, which they held in the right hand while they ate with the left. Mohammedans always eat with the left hand; in fact, each hand has its special duty assigned to it, and they never vary their habits.

Opposite the sand-bank was a small Malay house in among some coconut palms. I beckoned to Sahar and tried to persuade him to climb up and pick a nut.

He shook his head, but he crossed the stream, went into the house, and in a few moments returned with a monkey with a coil of string attached to its waist. The monkey had a very short tail, about half an inch long, but in other respects it was absurdly like Sahar. In about two minutes it was up the tree and looking down at us as much as to say: "Well, which nut do you want?" If Sahar had wanted the nut for making a curry, he would have said: "*Kuning* [yellow]," but as I wanted a drink, he said: "*Hijau* [green]," and immediately the monkey took hold of a large green coconut and spun it around until it dropped off the tree. This monkey is called the *brok* or coconut monkey, and the Malays for centuries have trained it to pick coconuts. In such a way probably originated the old traveller's tale that monkeys throw coconuts at people. Monkeys and apes certainly do break branches and sometimes pick jungle fruits and throw them down, but they usually do this when infuriated, and even then they do not throw them at people.

The coconut that the *brok* picked was considerably larger than my head. It was quite fascinating to see Sahar deftly cutting slices off one end of the husk with his sharp parang until he came to the coconut shell. Then Sahar repaid me for my joke, because he showed me the exposed shell and suddenly stuck his knife into it, and I got the milk straight in the eye. When the milk had stopped squirting out, Sahar cut a hole in the shell and handed me the best long drink I have ever had. I drank till I couldn't drink any more and then handed it to Sahar, but he shook his head and poured the rest of the milk on the ground. Most Malays will not drink coconut milk because they say it cools their amorous ardour, and when I got to know Sahar better I became convinced that he had never even tasted coconut milk. With one stroke of his knife he split the nut in half and then cut off a piece of the green husk which he carved into a spoon and handed me, beckoning me to eat the inside of the nut, which was full of a delicious jelly. It is this jelly that slowly turns into the hard white coconut with which most people are familiar. Sometimes, upon opening a ripe coconut, a ball of soft, spongy pith is found, about the size of an orange, which is delicious to eat. Sahar pointed out to me several coconuts hanging up in a tree which were sprouting. When the Malays plant a coconut, they first hang it up in the air for two or three months until a little tree commences to grow; then they dig a hole in the ground and at the bottom place a handful of salt. The coconut is placed on the salt, earth is rammed around it, and all that is necessary then is to wait for about eight years.

I do not think that any one ever saw a perfectly straight coconut palm; they are nearly always bent, and sometimes have a right-angle bend in the middle of the trunk. There are frequently steps cut into the tree all the way up. These steps are put there to enable Indians to climb up easily. They go up the tree, not to pick coconuts, but to tap the tree for toddy. In the Philippines, the sap of the coconut palm when fermented is called *tuba*, but it has the same effect in both places.

All the foliage and the fruit come from one bud. The tree usually has seventeen leaves, sometimes eighteen, and at the base of the leaves is what the Malays call *umbut*; this is the heart of the tree and is very sweet and crisp, and makes a delicious salad, but alas! to remove the *umbut* kills the tree. A coconut tree cannot be killed by ring-barking, because it doesn't have any bark.

Sahar and I returned to the boat, and as we continued the journey upstream, I amused myself by target shooting with my 22-bore rifle. Numerous fish traps lined the river bank. These traps were all very ingeniously made, with their mouths facing downstream, and were so designed that if a fish entered the trap it released a trigger which allowed a door to fall and shut in the fish.

Malays are enthusiastic followers of Izaak Walton

but they are frightfully lazy. I remember seeing an old Malay paddling along with about a dozen fishing rods in his boat. Every now and then he stopped and stuck a rod into the river bank, bent it almost into a semi-circle, attached a trigger, and left the hook dangling in the water. Then, too lazy to wait for a bite, he would go home and probably sleep. If a fish bit, the trigger went off, the rod straightened, and pulling the fish out left it hanging on the hook till the fisherman returned at sunset. Malays are usually referred to as the "Gentlemen of the East" because they are very polite, very independent, and usually well dressed, and they scarcely ever do any work. During my six years in Malay, I saw innumerable ways of fishing, but perhaps the most ingenious was the one by which we caught our supper that night.

About five o'clock we landed on the river bank and went to a small pond some twenty feet in diameter and four feet deep. Four of the Malays waded into the pond, each man holding in his hand a parang, which is a large knife about a foot long. They stirred up the mud with their feet until suddenly I noticed the nose of a fish rise above the surface of the water. Like lightning Sahar's parang flashed out and a moment later he picked up a fine fish weighing about a pound. Sahar's success excited the other Malays who, yelling and splashing about in the filthy water, caused the fish to come to the surface so quickly that in a few minutes we had far more than we could possibly eat. I saw an immense jungle tree not long after this, about two hundred feet high, with queer-looking brown objects hanging upon the lower branches, nearly a hundred feet from the ground. I shot at them with a rifle and every time I hit one it turned white. Then it gradually turned brown again, and I discovered that the objects were huge honey-combs, some of them six feet long. They were covered with bees, and when the bees were disturbed, they flew away and exposed the white comb that hung upon the tree. As the bees returned, the comb gradually turned brown again!

That night I saw a demonstration of insect organization which I believe is impossible to explain. It was a beautiful night and the air was full of extraordinary fireflies. About every fifteen minutes these flies separated into two armies, one settling on the trees growing on the left bank of the river and the other on the right bank. Then when I had decided that they had gone to bed for the night, the whole army on the left bank gave one big flash in perfect unison, which was immediately answered by another big flash from the right bank. There must have been thousands of them stretching along the river banks for a hundred yards or more, but the flies at one end of the line

Shortly before I took this photograph the little boy had eaten an enormous meal of rice. His mother had a private bathroom—you can see her head sticking over the top.

flashed their lights exactly at the same time as the flies at the other end, and the illumination was so strong that the branches of the trees could be seen quite distinctly.

I was awakened the next morning exactly at sunrise by the noise of the coolies clearing their throats and washing themselves in the river. It was wonderfully cool as I lay there under the mosquito net in the boat, watching the swiftly running river. The atmosphere was rosy, and there was a snowy mist covering the water. Just opposite was a path leading down the steep bank, and moored in the river was a raft upon which was a small hut without a roof. Inside the hut, a Malay woman was taking a bath, and I could see her head over the side of the bathroom. Standing waist deep in the river were several Malay girls bathing, but the instant they saw my head peep out from under the mosquito net, they hurriedly scrambled up the river bank.

Unmarried Malay girls are kept very much in the background except upon one day in the year called Hari Raya, when they come out in all their best clothes and spend the day feasting and paying visits. Hari Raya is the greatest Malay holiday, coming immediately after the Mohammedan fasting month of Ramadan. Ramadan is observed more or less strictly by all Malays; in fact, the really good Mohammedans not only fast all day but they refrain from swallowing their own saliva; consequently there is an unpleasant amount of spitting. The fasting day is spent chiefly in sleep, but at night they eat, drink, and make sleep impossible for other people by praying, which once heard is never forgotten; some people call it "dog howling," but they yell at the top of their voices, and if a man thinks he has a lovely voice he yells incessantly all night.

That morning I saw high up in the trunk of a dead tree a large hole through which was pouring a constant stream of bees, some entering, others leaving. As I watched them, I was astonished to see emerge from the beehive and dive into the river ahead of us a wonderful pink, green, and blue kingfisher. He looked like a jewel as he flashed from the hive into the sunlight and splashed in and then out of the water, carrying in his beak a small fish. With this he flew straight to the old tree and disappeared into the beehive again. "He's clever," said Sahar and he obviously was, because the bees took no notice of their lodger, and I'm certain no human being would have willingly robbed that bird's nest. Of course, the bird may have been there before the bees, and the bees may have decided to prepare a new kind of honey flavoured with fish—you never can tell!

Speaking of birds! What about Wallace's "Maleo"?

Here is a Malayan bird that is about as big as an ordinary fowl and lays an egg almost as big as itself which it places upright in a large hole in the sand, covers with sand, and leaves for the sun to hatch. Occasionally it lays its egg in a hole close to a hot spring for the necessary warmth. As soon as the egg hatches, out flies the chick into a neighbouring tree. It has grown its wings inside the egg and has already become independent.

But if you find these facts about jungle birds hard to believe I wonder what you will think about some of the jungle spiders. Mark Twain said that a spider in Bermuda once stole his boots, but here in the Malayan jungle, some of the spiders, I believe, not only could have stolen his boots but could have eaten them, too. I saw one spider's web so strong that when it touched my head it knocked my hat off. I had to cut it down with my knife in order to pass by. And one day I saw up in a tree on the side of the river a big spider who had decided that he wanted to go across without wetting his feet. He was spinning out a single thread, which the wind was blowing across the river. I could see the beautiful silver thread getting longer and longer, wafted well above the water, until it touched a tree on the opposite bank. Then the spider walked across on his own private bridge to explore the jungle on the other side.

About five o'clock in the evening, we came to a clearing on the river bank, in the middle of which were three Malay houses, built side by side, and joined to one another. There were several boats moored to the bank, and a neat staircase made of logs led up from the water. The boatmen exclaimed, "*Tûan suda sampai* [the master has arrived]," and I scrambled out of the boat. As I landed on the river bank, the first things that met my eye were countless chickens, with which I was to become familiar. These three picturesque houses, although built of palm leaves and perched on piles in true Malay fashion, constituted my first survey camp, a great contrast to the camps on the Grand Trunk Pacific Railway. The fronts of the houses were quite open, except for a low railing, disclosing three canvas tents pitched inside the houses. The middle house was evidently an office, because as I approached, a man looked up from a drawing board at which he was working. He was dressed in Malay costume, with bare feet, and had a long drooping moustache He looked as if he were in the last stages of consumption. His cheek bones seemed bursting through the skin and his eyes were sunken deep in the sockets. He invited me up into the house, and as I shook hands I noticed that his hand was as cold as ice and that his teeth were chattering. "My name is Yorkshire; I am the locating engineer; I've got a touch of this bloody fever," he said. "I suppose you are the new engineer! I hope they haven't sent me another one of those useless——!"

Turning from me, he called, out, "Siti! Siti!" and to my astonishment there appeared from the next room a very pretty barefoot Malay girl, dressed in gorgeous silk clothing, wearing heavy gold anklets and a lot of gold jewellery which, like her teeth, was stained red. "My God! I've been in this bloody jungle for fifteen years, and the only things that keep me alive are Siti and the Sydney *Bulletin!*" Yorkshire exclaimed as he indicated a magazine with a bright pink cover. He spoke to Siti in Malay. She glanced at me shyly and disappeared from the room.

I handed Yorkshire my introduction from the head office, which he read and exclaimed: "Thank the Lord they have sent me someone with American experience; I'm an Austrilian and we railroad in the American way." It is not generally known that an Australian is a very rare person; the majority of Australia's inhabitants being Austrilians to whom "cake" is "kyke."

The scene in the tent that evening would have astonished my relations and friends if they could have seen Yorkshire and me as we sprawled on the beautifully woven Malay mats that covered the floor, smoking, while Siti played quaint Malay tunes on a German accordion in the soft yellow light of an oil lamp.   Outside, the darkness was so intense that it seemed dreadful, and I was relieved when Siti ordered Yorkshire to build a camp fire outside.   When it was blazing fiercely, Yorkshire winked at me and said, "*Rimau ta mau mari ini malum* [A tiger won't want to come around to-night]."   Siti instantly snapped out: "*Jangan! gila betul!* [Don't! You are certainly crazy!]"   and I learned that a tiger is never to be mentioned by name in the jungle.   Malays, especially women, are terrified of tigers, and the animal is generally only referred to in terms of respect, such as "his lordship," or perhaps "the old gentleman."   To mention the word *rimau* or tiger is to run the risk of being heard by the animal and promptly devoured.

Yorkshire was a veritable gold mine for tiger tales; he told me the experience of a girl who had recently come out to Malay as a hospital nurse.   Her bungalow was situated on the very edge of the jungle.   One night, being unable to sleep on account of the oppressive heat in the house, she dragged her bed to the window, opened the shutters, and dropped off to sleep with the cool night breeze blowing upon her. Suddenly she awakened to hear something scratching on the outside of the house, and as she watched the window, there slowly appeared the huge head of a tiger. The girl did not scream, but snatching up her pillow she threw it at him and hit him square in the face. The tiger caught the pillow in his paws and with a snarl began to eat it; but the pillow was full of feathers which went down his throat and he was almost tickled to death, apparently, because, spluttering and sneezing, he fell out of the window backward and began clawing at his mouth to get rid of the feathers, while the girl rushed to the back of the house and fetched a watchman who killed him.

One of the best tiger stories I ever heard was related to me first hand and I have every reason to believe it. A young engineer was sent up a mountain in the jungle to take some astronomical observations. After an absence of several days, he arrived in camp one night in his pajamas, which were torn to pieces, and here is the story that he told his chief.

"Last night I decided to sleep out in the open because my tent was so hot. I suspended my mosquito net from the branch of a tree and placed my camp bed under it and went to sleep. The night was pitch-dark and I slept soundly until I felt something hot blowing upon my face. Immediately I waked and saw two fiery eyes looking at me through the mosquito net. They came closer and closer until they actually touched the net, and then suddenly they began going round and round my bed. A moment afterward, another pair of eyes joined the first and began encircling my bed until I couldn't stand it any longer; I gave a frightful yell and sprang out of bed. The eyes immediately disappeared and here I am. That hill swarms with tigers." The story sounded so incredible that the next morning the chief of the party decided to investigate. Upon reaching the hill-top, he found the deserted camp, the bed under the tree, and the suspended mosquito net, just as had been described, and all around the camp bed was a ring of thick black mud. Pressed into the mud were dozens of tiger tracks and there was no doubt at all that one or more tigers had been walking round and round the bed watching the man within the net. Every now and then the tiger stopped his march and sniffed at the man; but as soon as the mosquito net touched his nose he became nervous and began once more his tramp around the bed. Finally, when the man yelled and jumped out of bed, the tiger fled in terror!

One of our own coolies, Mat, an unusually fine specimen of a man, was carried off by a tiger in a most extraordinary way. He was sleeping in a house with twelve other Malays, all lying in a row upon a bench raised a few inches from the ground. Mat was exactly in the middle of the row, and there were six men between him and the door of the house. The night passed in perfect quietness, but when the roll call was held in the morning, Mat didn't answer, and the coolies stated that his place was vacant when they woke up. At first we thought that he had gone down to the river, but when he didn't turn up we examined the ground near the house and found tiger tracks leading from the door to the jungle, and after following them for a quarter of a mile we found Mat's legs, arms, and head. The tiger had walked over six sleeping men and chosen the finest. We decided to move camp that day.

When I told Yorkshire of my experience with Sahar, he recommended that I should appoint him my personal "boy," whose duty it would be to wait upon me hand and foot in return for a salary of seven dollars a month. The next morning when I opened my eyes, Sahar was standing close beside the bed and when he saw that I was wide awake he said, "*Makanan tay, tûan?* [Tea, sir?]" How long he had been standing beside the bed with a tray of tea in his hand I cannot tell, but all the time I was in Malaya I never remember being actually called or awakened by a Malay servant. They consider it dangerous to waken a sleeping person because they believe that during sleep the body and soul are separated and that an attempt to awaken a person suddenly might result in instant death; so they wait patiently until their presence close to a sleeper awakens him gradually.

When I got out of bed, I found my clothes neatly laid out, and in a few moments I was dressed in a khaki suit, puttees, and canvas boots, ready for my first work in the jungle. As I entered the dining room, I saw Yorkshire hurl a plate and a roast chicken at his Chinese cook, and with a true flow of Austrilian blasphemy he instructed the terrified man not to give him any more "dead hen," meaning chicken.

"*Mana teloar?* [Where are the eggs?]" Yorkshire roared.

"*Teloar tiada, tûan* [There ain't no eggs, sir]," said the cook, trembling.

"What!" shrieked Yorkshire. "Three hundred bloody chickens and no eggs!" and turning to me he explained what I afterward discovered to be true, that it is always necessary to buy eggs from the cook no matter how many fowls one may keep, because the cook always sees to it that no eggs shall ever be found in the fowl house, swearing by all that a Chinaman holds sacred that the chickens never lay. Thus he derives a private income from them himself.

Yorkshire was evidently in a bad temper this morning, because again he thundered: *"Brapa akor, ayam?* [How many chickens are there?]"

"About a hundred, sir," replied the now terrified cook. "——! ——! ——!" yelled Yorkshire furiously. "You thief! You not only sell me my own eggs but you sell me the same chickens about a dozen times over! *Pergi! bilang semoar, lekas!* [Go! count them, quick!]" and as the cook dashed out, Yorkshire followed him to the fowl house.

In crawled the cook and soon a perfect shower of chickens came tumbling out. Each fowl as it fell on the ground promptly lay on its back decorously, with its feet sticking in the air and its neck craned into an absurd position so that the wretched bird was looking between its legs. Then I noticed that each bird had its wings crossed and locked on its back, which caused it to assume of its own accord this upside-down position.

"There is one that has been struck by lightning," said Yorkshire as a chicken arrived with all its feathers growing on backward, even its wing feathers.

"Look! There is Tatcho!" he exclaimed as a large fowl came out, perfectly naked, not even a hair, and walked about looking absurd and wagging its bald extremity.

"He is tame," said Yorkshire as he picked up the

naked fowl and handed him to me. From its appearance I had expected it to be cold and clammy but it was hot and I dropped it.

It is very strange to see the extraordinary freaks that Malay chickens have produced by constant inbreeding. Eventually we counted about a hundred chickens of all sizes, shapes, colours, breeds, and both sexes. This occasional checking up puts a stop temporarily to the cook's profiteering.

After the chicken roll call came that of the coolies. Yorkshire and I stood on the veranda of our house while the assembled Malays stood without. They were an extraordinary crowd of people, including young boys immaculately dressed in Malay *baju* or shirt and big baggy trousers, and old boys dressed in filthy jungle rags much more suitable for the day's work. Most of them were smoking. All of them carried *parangs* or jungle knives; some had *bliongs*, or native axes, as well, while the smartest-looking ones were carrying the various kinds of surveying instruments. There were evidently two separate gangs of about twelve men, each in charge of a *mandor*, or a headman. As Yorkshire read over the names, the *mandor* answered, and it was extremely funny to hear them. There were so many Jesuses and Mahomets that they had to be numbered Jesus,

1, 2, and 3; besides these names there were Abrahams, Josephs, Jacobs, Noahs, and many Moseses.

I often am asked by people after lectures to cut out reference to Malays who are called after Jesus, but I cannot understand why Christians need be ashamed that Mohammedans call their children after Jesus just as we call ours after Peter and Paul. It is awfully inconvenient when you have a cook called Jesus and he can't cook!

Yorkshire handed over to me one of the gangs in charge of a *mandor* named Hussein, while he instructed his own *mandor* to go upstream to the town of Kuala Lipis and find a Chinese cook for me, and also to get the mail.

CHAPTER VII

OF ALL my varied experiences in the Malay Peninsula, I think that the one that made the most impression upon my mind was my first day's engineering work in the jungle. Yorkshire and I had separate boats. Heavy rain had evidently fallen during the night in the mountains because the river was swollen, and as soon as we pushed off from the bank, our boats were swirled away down the stream. I saw Yorkshire seize a paddle and heard him yell; his coolies instantly began paddling frantically. I myself was seized with the same excitement, I also gave a yell and there followed the most exciting boat race I have ever taken part in.

Malays usually regard any one who paddles a boat down the stream as crazy, but when there is a race in prospect their sporting instinct is aroused. I paddled and shouted like mad as my boat passed the two laden with coolies and began to creep up on Yorkshire's. Just when victory seemed within our reach a most amazing thing happened. Ahead of us and swimming swiftly across the river was a water-snake about three feet long. The snake was making straight for

Yorkshire's boat when the coolies noticed it, ceased their paddling, and began beating the water with their paddles. They managed to drive off the snake, which passed the stern of Yorkshire's boat, hesitated for a moment, and made toward mine. It was our turn to start beating the water, but the snake somehow or other got into the boat, and immediately there was a wild stampede to opposite ends of the boat. The snake appeared slightly bewildered, but after contemplating us, it calmly slipped over the side of the boat and continued its journey across the river.

I had similar experiences with water-snakes on several occasions, and the Malays say that a water-snake never swims across a river without inspecting every obstacle in its path, no matter whether it is a boat, a log of wood, or a man swimming.

After the excitement had died down we paddled along slowly, following Yorkshire's boat to a spot on the river bank where we all landed. By landing, I do not mean just getting out of the boat on to the bank, but pulling ourselves ashore by hanging on to jungle creepers, then by slashing our way individually through the dense undergrowth that covered the steep bank. In fact, the land sloped into the river at about fifty degrees, and it was almost like scrambling up the face of a precipice. After climbing up about fifty feet, we came out into a clearing some thirty feet wide but still at that unpleasant slope of fifty degrees. In the middle of the space was a wooden post about four inches square and two feet high, which denoted the end of the surveyed portion of the railway. Looking back along the side of the hill I could see only about forty feet each way because the ground was rising even more steeply longitudinally than it was transversely.

I thought to myself, "What a place for a railroad!" As a matter of fact, the roadbed had to be kept in place by retaining walls. After recovering his breath Yorkshire turned to me and said, "Well! There you are! Walk back along the clearing about a quarter of a mile and start levelling from there to this spot!"

The night before I had been telling Yorkshire that in Canada I frequently did six miles of levelling a day, and here he was telling me to do only a quarter of a mile! Off I started scrambling up hill and down dale, accompanied by five coolies.

Very soon I began to perspire so profusely that in a few minutes I was literally wet through. My khaki clothes looked black and water was running off my chin in a continual stream. Upon reaching the spot where Yorkshire had instructed me to start work, the coolie who was carrying the levelling instrument handed it to me, and while I was adjusting it he opened a large Chinese umbrella and held it over me.

Nothing is more delightful than to lie on a mattress underneath the sunshade and be poled up a Malay river.

Then my troubles began, because I could not speak
Malay and had to give all my instructions in panto-
mime.   As the sun rose higher, the level got hotter
until the spirit bubble had shrunk to about one tenth
its normal size.   Every time I made an entry in my
level notebook, a perfect stream of perspiration poured
over the book and smudged the figures.

I had expected to do that quarter of a mile's work
in about half an hour, but it actually took me five
hours, and when I reached camp late in the afternoon, burnt red as a lobster, dirty, and smarting from
the bites of numerous insects, with blood running out
of my boots from over-gorged leeches in my socks, I
was greeted by Yorkshire, cool as a cucumber, dressed
in Malay costume, and Siti, who shouted something
at me in Malay that I could not understand but which
caused my coolies to laugh.

Yorkshire exclaimed, "Hello!   I thought you were
lost; you had better have a bath and lunch."   Not a
word did he say about the levelling job he had given
me; nor did I.   I climbed up the steps into my
house, where Sahar took off my boots and puttees.
In between every fold of the puttees was a leech, and
I was kept busy with a box of matches torturing those
beastly bloodsuckers.   The Malay jungle swarms with
them, and they are especially numerous after rain,
yet they drown when thrown into a pool.   In size

they vary from tiny mites about a sixteenth of an inch in length to good healthy ones, two inches long. They are about as big as a match before they bite you and as large as a cigar afterward. So clever are they in biting that it is rarely they are noticed until they are so fat that they feel like little cold jelly bags hanging on to your body. I used to test a leech's sense of smell by carrying it fifteen yards away and leaving it on the ground while I returned to my seat. The leech would stand on end, waving himself about, scenting the air in every direction. Then without the slightest hesitation he would make a bee line for me. As soon as he reached me, he would quiver with excitement, then climb up and get through the eyelet of my boot. By a providential arrangement, leeches go to bed at night; I doubt whether, if they did not, there would be many animals in the jungle.

As soon as I had undressed, I had a hot bath and then a delicious lunch, consisting of olives, sardines, oxtail soup, roast chicken, peaches and cream. Everything except the chicken was canned, and I was especially interested in the milk, which was ordinary cow's milk, but not condensed or evaporated in any way. Both Borden's and Nestlé's export this milk to tropical countries, and it is exactly like fresh milk with all the cream on it, but I have never been able to buy it in America and thus convince people that I really mean ordinary milk and not evaporated or condensed.

After luncheon, Yorkshire, Siti, and I often used to go for a stroll along a jungle path to visit some Malay *kampong* or house of which Siti had heard. Siti was always dressed in her most gorgeous apparel and it was most amusing and interesting to observe that she was a personage of considerable importance in the eyes of other Malay women of less easy virtue.

It was on such visits as these that Siti became a real Malay again. She would squat down on the floor of a Malay house and start chewing betel nut while the hostess brought out various Malay delicacies or fruit, or opened the family chest and showed Siti the lovely silk clothes that practically every Malay has stored away for use on Hari Raya. After such a walk he would return laden with fruit, or with some new pet such as a cat or a monkey or a *serindit*, the beautiful little Malay parrakeet.

Malays like cats, and they are looked upon more or less as sacred and never to be killed. If a cat steals the chickens or makes itself in any way objectionable it is tied to a raft and started floating down a river, so that although it is successfully got rid of, no particular person can be accused of actually killing it!

One day I went out fishing with Siti, who was a most enthusiastic follower of Izaak Walton. We were fishing in a small pond when her hook became entangled and she waded out to free it. I happened to notice a large buffalo leech called by Malays a *linta* swimming toward her and called out, "*Linta!*"

With a terrified shriek of "*Mana?* [Where?]" she dropped her rod and literally flung herself into the water toward me and scrambled out looking like a bedraggled cat. Malay women behave themselves in the presence of a *linta* like some white women in the presence of a mouse; but with good reason, because a *linta* is as big as a cigar before it bites you and as fat as a German sausage afterward.

It will be remembered that a boat had been sent upstream to the town of Kuala Lipis to fetch a cook for my own use. After four days the boat returned not only with a Chinese cook, but also with the cook's wife, a pair of turkeys which I promptly named Adam and Eve, and a wonderful little anthropoid ape, the smallest of her kind in the world, called a "gibbon." I called her "Rose of Sharon." The cook's name was Salleh and he was something of a character. Although a Cantonese by birth, he had married a Malay girl and turned Mohammedan. He had the usual trouble of the Chinese in pronouncing his r's, and when he wanted to say he was afraid we might be attacked by a *rimau*—a tiger—he called it "*limau*," or "lemon," but he was a marvellous cook, and within

Kuala Lipis where the river Lipis joins the Jelei; looking downstream.

fifteen minutes he could catch, kill, cook, and serve a chicken, including soup. Just for sport I watched him do the whole business one day, although he little knew that I was looking on.

I had surprised him by returning early to camp, before he had begun to prepare luncheon. When I yelled at him, "Boy, *siap makanan!* [Boy, get food ready!]" he immediately replied, "*Baik, tûan, makanan siap!* [All right, sir, food is ready!]"

A moment later I saw him, with some rice in his hand, squatting on the ground in the midst of about a hundred chickens. They were all quite tame, since they were used to being killed regularly three times a day. Salleh took hold of them and felt their breasts as they continued to feed out of his hand. Then there was a squawk—he had cut off a chicken's head. While the fowl was still beating its wings Salleh plunged it into hot water, which removed all its feathers. It was then drawn and quartered and while it was frying the giblets were boiling. Salleh next took a soup plate, peppered the bottom of it, put in a teaspoonful of Worcestershire sauce and about a dozen canned peas and added some of the hot water in which the giblets had been boiling. While I drank the soup, he opened a tin of sardines and a bottle of olives and served the next course. Finally he brought in the fried chicken. It was exactly fifteen minutes since the chicken had been walking about.

One day, when I was utterly tired of chicken, I asked Hussein what the coolies ate, and he answered, "*Daging, tûan*," which means, "Meat, sir." He then showed me fresh meat hanging on strings about their houses. "It's deer meat, sir," he said. "Do you want a deer?"

It sounded easy. I walked about two miles into the jungle with him. Then he took his knife and began to chop down some bushes to make a little hut. When it was finished, we both crawled into it and covered ourselves with leaves. As I stuck my gun through the side of the hut, I saw Hussein take out of his belt two little sticks about a foot long. Next he picked a broad leaf, laid it on the ground, and rattled upon it with the sticks making a noise like the "brr" of a drum. When he had repeated the call two or three times he said, "Look, sir," and I saw coming out of the jungle a deer.

Again Hussein beat his leaf, "brr." This time the deer came right out into the open, looked for a large leaf, put his feet upon it and rattled it with his hoofs, making exactly the same sort of challenging noise. Hussein replied and man and deer began an alternate drumming. Each time the deer came a bit closer, and when at last I fired, I could not help hitting him.

I ran out of the hut, picked him up, and put him into my pocket. I fried him in a frying pan that evening. He was a perfect little deer, only seven inches high, with a body about the size of a small rabbit, legs as thick as a pencil, and dainty cloven hoofs. Though he was without antlers, he had in his upper jaw two very sharp tusks more than an inch long and curved almost into a semi-circle. Hussein told me that, when this deer is chased by a tiger or a leopard and finds himself hard pressed, he jumps into the air, hangs to the branch of a small tree by means of his little tusks, and pretends to be a fruit! He is not the *rusa* or *sambur* deer, or the *kijang*, or barking deer, but the *plandok*, the mouse deer, which is as popular in Malay folklore as the fox is in Western fairy tales.

Hussein was an old-timer at railroading and he had an unusual knowledge of jungle craft. The Malays as a people do not live in the jungle but upon the banks of rivers or on the sea coast, sometimes actually building their villages in the sea. The jungle is regarded with superstitious awe and dread, not only on account of tigers, but because of the ghosts and evil spirits that are supposed to be in it. When they have to enter the jungle for some purpose of their own, they invariably go with companions, and usually either privately or publicly call upon the spirits of the jungle to inform them that they intend no harm but are merely entering the jungle for some harmless purpose and of course with the greatest respect for its unearthly inhabitants.

Practically all the main paths through the jungle used by men are ancient or modern elephant tracks. Very often there are side and branch tracks, and I noted, whenever we passed one, how careful Hussein was to cut down a small sapling and place it across the side track as an indication to any one following that we had not gone that way. Many of these elephant tracks are marked on the map and I have surveyed several hundred miles of them. Sometimes a huge tree falls across a track, the log being perhaps eight feet thick. A new track is then cut all around the tree for elephants, while a staircase is built over the log for pedestrians. By the side of the staircase, someone usually starts cutting a notch in the trunk and then each person using the staircase cuts a little more until the tree log is cut clean through and the old track is once more opened through the huge notch in the log.

Such places have their disadvantages, especially when, as sometimes happens, an elephant comes along with its baby. Hussein told me that once he saw a mother elephant and her baby arrive at such an obstruction.   The wise old mother carefully tried the size of the notch and decided to walk all around the prostrate tree, but young master elephant, no doubt suffering from *dementia præcox*, like most youths, decided to pass through the hole, made a dash at it, and became firmly wedged in the middle, with his trunk on one side of the tree and his tail on the other, both wagging frantically.   The more he struggled, the tighter he became wedged.   Terrified, he began squealing for his mother.

By this time the mother had reached the other side of the tree, and hearing her son's distress, she walked up and carefully contemplated his ridiculous situation.   After a moment's thought, she turned around and retraced her steps to the other side of the tree, put down her head and with a rush and a thud bumped master elephant and shot him clean through the hole and he went on his way rejoicing.

The first few weeks of my jungle experience were in company with Yorkshire, who taught me the art of surveying under the peculiar conditions that exist in such dense vegetation.   He told me that many a young engineer gave it up as a bad job when he found it impossible to see more than a few yards ahead.   In fact, I am convinced that to be a successful surveyor in the jungle it is absolutely necessary to have one's sense of direction acutely developed, and in this respect Yorkshire was an extraordinary man.

He would start out by himself, with an aneroid in one hand and a sharp parang in the other, cutting his way whenever necessary, and soon would be lost to sight and sound. I would wait perhaps two hours, and then Yorkshire would return, either cursing profusely or quietly satisfied, and say to me, "Cut ahead about half a mile, then bear off to the left until you cross a stream, then turn sharp to the right and keep straight on." In this way he would indicate for me three or four days' hard work, and he was rarely wrong in his location.

Few people have a correct idea of the appearance of the jungle inside. In these immense forests of the tropical rain regions, the decay of vegetable matter during countless ages has enriched the soil to a depth of many feet, and from it has sprung a marvellous tangle of vegetation. Huge trees, shrubs, bushes, underwood, thorns, creepers, climbing plants and trailing vines all struggle to reach the light.

Trees with lateral branches are rarely seen, but instead, they shoot up straight and smooth for a hundred feet before branching out into a large cabbage-like top. Ferns, mosses, orchids, and other parasitic plants in countless variety cover the trees from top to bottom. Immense rope-like vines passing from tree to tree, up and down, some of them 600 feet long, bind the jungle into one big tangle.

Orchid plants abound on every side, but to the observer on the ground their blossoms (like other flowers) are conspicuous by their absence. If only the jungle could be examined from an aëroplane, its beauty and wonderful colours would be seen in their full glory because the tops of the trees are often ablaze with masses of blossom.

I happened once to be engaged upon the sinking of a number of wells in the jungle, which when filled up with concrete were to act as foundations for a bridge, and in one instance I remember that the well cut through more than a hundred feet of decaying vegetable matter and was impeded at that depth by a huge half-decomposed log. With such a soil combined with a shade temperature of 82 degrees F. and a sun temperature of 160, together with an annual rainfall varying from 150 to 250 inches, it is not surprising that Nature in this part of the world has produced a jungle instead of an ordinary forest.

It was three years before I could even begin to emulate Yorkshire's example, but when I did, and when I was alone and independent of him, I found this solitary penetrating into places that had never been trodden by a man the most fascinating work I had ever done. The sensation of being absolutely alone in apparent safety but knowing all the time that a dozen different kinds of death lurked on every side was in itself thrilling and exciting.

One day I wandered off into the jungle by myself and was about to cut down a palm leaf that was obstructing my way, when I stopped instinctively and saw within six inches of my face a small green snake with its head waving from side to side.   I was so surprised and shocked that I just stood still and stared at it. To my astonishment, although I was watching the snake intently, it disappeared silently and mysteriously, blending cleverly with the surrounding foliage.

As a matter of fact, snakes are not seen as often as people think, but I will never forget my first meeting with a python.   It was about eleven o'clock one morning and I had purposely gone ahead of the coolies when, suddenly, I almost stepped on a huge snake that was coiled up in a pool of water.   I watched it as it slept, its body rising and falling in the water with every breath.   As nearly always happens when you meet an animal unexpectedly in the jungle, I had left my gun for one of the coolies to carry, but I retired about ten feet back into the undergrowth and fired all five chambers of my revolver at the snake.   Whether I hit him I don't know, but he uncoiled like a huge spring.   It is said that a whale has no vocal organs, but that it can

Orchid plants are common in the jungle, but blossoms are rather conspicuous by their absence, except on the top of the jungle.

make a noise like a cow! Well—this python distinctly gave a horrible grunt as, like lightning, he uncoiled and rapidly glided away into the gloom of the forest. His head must have been at least two feet from the ground and his body was as thick as a man's thigh.

When I returned to my coolies I found them scraping off leeches, and the ground was covered with big splotches of blood. We seemed to have struck a district where these jungle pests literally swarmed in thousands. Nothing would keep them out! They crawled through the eyelets of my boots, up my clothes, and down my neck.

One afternoon our whole party was completely disorganized by an attack of giant wasps called *tebuan*. We were walking along an elephant track when Hussein yelled, *"Tebuan!"* Instantly the whole party except the wise old men scattered. Baggage was thrown away as we were individually chased by big black-and-red wasps, at least four times as big as the domestic ones in this country. Every now and then could be heard an agonized yell as one of them left his visiting card on some unfortunate coolie. I had been dragged down by Hussein who whispered fiercely, *"Diam!"* I thought he had been stung until I realized that the word meant "be quiet." It is all very well to say "be quiet" when two or three huge wasps are crawling over you with their wings buzzing in fury, but I thought of bee-keepers at home with swarms of bees crawling over them and I kept quiet. After ten minutes that seemed like eternity the wasps had gone and the coolies began to come back, some of them with big ears, others with an eye closed, and one so badly stung that I had to doctor him considerably.

After a while the time came when Yorkshire decided that I was capable of running my own party, and he instructed me to proceed up the river to a place called Kuala Tanum. "Kuala" means the junction of two rivers, and "Kuala Tanum" is where the river Tanum runs into the river Jelei.

CHAPTER VIII

I WAS not at all sorry when I started out for Kuala Tanum with twelve coolies in charge of Hussein in two boats. Sahar carried the cat, Salleh and his wife carried Adam and Eve, the turkeys, while Rose of Sharon walked. We also had about a hundred chickens packed like sardines in baskets.

Each boat was poled by four coolies and in the leading boat was Salleh and the menagerie. He hated the river and couldn't swim an inch, which unfortunate failing gave him a most exciting experience the same afternoon. It had been thundering heavily since 11 o'clock in the morning although the sky was bright and clear, and when I noticed large pieces of foam floating past our boat I knew that there was a great storm in progress in the mountains.

To my astonishment, with only this momentary warning, the river began to rise so rapidly that several small islets ahead of us disappeared completely in less than half an hour and soon all kinds of strange objects began floating down the stream. Logs, old clothes, a bathing house complete, coconut shells

galore, and several large trees passed us.   Soon poling became impossible, and following the example of
the coolies in Salleh's boat ahead of us we drew into
the river bank and slowly made our way upstream by
pulling at the overhanging branches that were trailing
in the water.   Someone in the boat ahead gave a
yell and as I looked up I saw all the coolies, Salleh's
wife, and Salleh jump into the river.   The cook was
hanging on to the edge of the boat with his right arm
and as he drifted near us we rescued him and the boat.

One by one the others swam back like dogs, and
I learnt the reason for the unexpected bathing party.
In pulling at the branches one of the coolies disturbed
a large snake which fell into the boat and started
floundering about in the bilge water.   Salleh told me
that after the snake had made several unsuccessful
attempts to climb up the slippery side of the boat it
noticed Salleh's arm, crawled up it and over his
shoulder into the river!   As the reptile was doubtless
just as scared as Salleh it never thought of biting
him but only of escape.

After two days' hard work we reached Kuala
Tanum where we landed and at once commenced to
build a new camp on the land between the two rivers
at the very junction.   While the coolies were making
the camp, I called upon the Rajah of Kuala Tanum
whose name was Wan Chi.   His house was situated

The Rajah of Kuala Tanum, Wan Chi, and his "lice," as he called them. "They are my relatives," he explained. "They live on me!"

close to my camp, and when I approached, a rather stout middle-aged Malay met me.

He was dressed in full Malay costume, including trousers, and wore in his belt a kris, but the latter could only be assumed to be there, because it was carefully veiled by a fold of his sarong.   After the usual "*Tabay, tûan. Apa kaba?* [I salute you, sir. What news?]" he introduced himself to me as the Rajah's brother, and told me that his name was Wan Lela.

He said that the Rajah was asleep but would see me in the afternoon.   Wan Lela took out of his pocket two very fine tiger claws and presented them to me. I took him back to camp and gave him a tin of Egyptian cigarettes, much to his delight.   But after smoking two, he informed me that he was *mabu*—drunk! He told me that if I would like to have the tiger claws mounted, he had some native gold, and produced a small box of tiny nuggets.   I returned the claws and about a month afterward a messenger arrived in camp with them, beautifully set in pure gold and ornamented with Malay filigree work.

That afternoon I had tea with Wan Lela and Wan Chi.   I happened to take with me my double-barrelled shotgun, and the Rajah requested me to take his photograph with him holding the gun. While I was arranging the two brothers, about ten other Malays lined up behind the Rajah.

I said to him: "Who are these?"

And Wan Chi whispered: "My lice!"

My face no doubt showed some surprise at the unexpected answer, because he quickly qualified the statement by saying: "They are my relations; they live on me."

After the photo was taken, we entered Wan Chi's house which was Malay outside but looked like a cheap Chinese café inside, being ruined by chairs and round tables, probably purchased from some sale of restaurant furniture.

Wan Chi was anxious for me to see his son and heir, who in a few moments was brought in by his mother. He was a little fellow about four years old, rather shy, almost white, and dressed in gorgeous Malay costume. I strongly suspected that he was more used to running about naked because, when his mother stood him upon a table in order to show him off to better advantage, his little yellow trousers fell down around his ankles, without causing him the least embarrassment.

While we were sitting at tea, I noticed a boatload of Malays, about nine men, women, and children, all dressed in marvellous colours, pass up the Tanum River, and the heavy boatload was being poled upstream by only one man.

He was about four feet, six inches in height, almost black, with woolly hair, and very muscular.

Wan Chi, noticing my surprise, said: "*Orang utan, tûan! Kerja kuat!* [A jungle man, sir! He works hard!]"

To naturalists, the word *orang-utan* means the great ape of Borneo, but the Malays call the ape *mias* and refer to the aboriginal jungle dwarfs as *orang utan*: *orang*—man; *utan*—jungle. Very few white people have ever seen them in their wild state, but the Malays have hunted and enslaved them for centuries. Many Europeans who have lived for years in the Malay Peninsula have only a vague idea of what the country contains besides tin, rubber, and coconuts. A great many of them divide the natives of the country into two classes: Malays and Sakais, the latter being the commonest and most familiar aborigines. As a matter of fact, volumes have been and still could be written concerning the other pagan races of Malay who are not Sakais at all.

The man I saw poling the boat was nothing like a Sakai, having instead of curly black hair tightly curled wool typical of the pure Negrito, and except for a small piece of bark, he was naked. I asked Wan Chi eagerly if it would be possible to see any of these jungle men, but he shook his head and said: "*Ta buleh jumpa, tûan; dia takut! Dia lari!* [You can't meet them, sir; they are frightened! They run away!]"

However, I kept to the subject and discovered that Wan Chi had a considerable amount of intercourse with them and that he did a lot of bartering. I noticed around his house huge piles of *rotan* and logs of strange coloured wood; also plenty of *damar*, which is a jungle sap largely used for making torches.

Although bartering occurred, the Malays rarely actually saw the jungle men, because the method of procedure was as follows: The Malays would leave, say, a bag of salt on the edge of the jungle one evening; the next morning the salt was gone and in its place would be its equivalent in jungle produce, for instance, gutta percha, *damar*, or *rotan*.

Some of the older Malays claimed to have had dealings directly with these wild people, and, in fact, one of them, named Mat Noh, could speak a few words of their primitive language. As soon as I discovered this, I sent him downstream with a note to Yorkshire, who gave the old man a contract to construct a series of survey camps for my use. When Mat Noh returned with his contract, he told me that he intended to use *orang utan* to cut the wood and other material for the houses.

The night before he left us to start on his contract

it happened to be raining very heavily. I was in the coolies' camp talking to them when Mat Noh started out into the rain with a flaming torch to hunt frogs. In a few minutes he returned with a large and lanky frog and very soon its hind legs were sizzling on the fire. The younger Malays wouldn't touch it, but old Mat Noh thoroughly relished the juicy titbit. When he had finished, he rolled himself a *roco*, or cigarette, made with the native tobacco and rolled in a leaf of nipa palm, and when the tobacco began to soothe his nerves, he became quite talkative.

One of the coolies asked him to tell a story. We all gathered around the fire, and while the rain roared upon the roof, Mat Noh gave us "The Legend of the Python" which explains how the snake obtained the wonderful pattern on its back and why its bite is not poisonous. After two or three deep whiffs of his cigarette, Mat Noh began:

"Once upon a time, long, long ago, when there were no poisonous snakes and the python was the king of reptiles, there lived a woman called Aunt Eve. One day the python, who was snow-white, met Eve and she asked the snake to live with her. After much persuasion, the python consented on condition that Eve knitted a pattern on his back in order to make him beautiful.

"Eve began and made the most beautiful patterns

on the snake's back, commencing from his tail. One day the work was finished and the python discovered that he was not only the most beautiful snake but that his bite had become intensely poisonous, so poisonous, in fact, that it was not necessary for him to bite a person in order to kill him, but merely to snap at his footsteps.

"This pleased him so much that he proceeded to snap at the footsteps of all his enemies. Soon, however, he began to doubt whether his enemies were really dead, and seeing a crow flying by, he asked him to find out whether all his enemies whose footsteps he had bitten were really dead.

"The crow flew away and passed over a village where a funeral was taking place, and the people, as is the custom amongst the Mohammedans, were rejoicing and making a great noise because the dead man, like all Mohammedans, had gone to heaven. Not understanding this, the crow returned to the python and reported that his enemies were laughing at him. This so enraged the python that he summoned the reptiles of the jungle to come and hear what he had to say. When they had all arrived, the python climbed up a very tall tree and addressed the others, saying: 'You all know that I am the only poisonous snake in the world.' And they replied: 'True, O King!' Then said the python: 'Behold, I have determined no longer to be poisonous.' And he spat out all his poison so that it went all over the tree, which itself became poisonous and is so to this day, and is called the Upas tree. As the poison dripped off the tree, many of the snakes who were envious of the python ate it themselves and became poisonous; even the frogs ate some, but were condemned to live in water for the rest of their lives in order to wash the poison away."

The next morning, Mat Noh started off to build a series of camps ahead of me, about six miles apart, and in the direction of Gunong Tahan (Forbidden Mountain), the highest peak in the Peninsula. As we left camp to start surveying up the Tanum River, I noticed Sahar hanging out my washing. Three hours afterward, when I returned to camp, there had been a shower of rain and I was obliged to take a boat right up to the house! Rose of Sharon was in a terrible state of excitement running around the house waving her arms in the air as she watched the water rising.

Just to see how deep the rain water was, I stepped out of the boat. The water came over my knees and I wondered what happened to the ants when a flood comes. My question was almost immediately answered when I noticed coming toward me on the surface of the water a big brown ball, about one foot in diameter. It was slowly turning over and over, and when I examined it I found that it was a solid ball of ants all clinging together for dear life and taking it in turns to have a ducking! Soon the ball touched a tree trunk and immediately the ants climbed up into the tree and saved their lives!

I have never seen so many different kinds of ants as in the Malay jungle. Some were so tiny that they could scarcely be seen, while others were more than an inch long and stood half an inch high. Mr. Roy Chapman Andrews told me that when he was in Borneo he had great difficulty in catching animals in his traps because the Malayan ants were so huge that one of them was sufficient to spring a trap, and as the ants invariably found the traps before the larger animals did, trapping was seriously interfered with.

One day when I was standing beside a large tree, amusing myself by cutting off slices of the bark, I uncovered a hollow in the tree in which there were ten large ants about half an inch long. They looked lovely and silky, but instead of rushing aimlessly about the way most ants do, these stood still. No doubt the sudden removal of the bark covering their home surprised them, but they were evidently ready for any emergency. Taking my pocketknife I opened the large blade and slowly moved the point toward them. When it was about two inches from them they lined up into absolutely straight rows and, as if at a word of command, simultaneously bent their bodies double and squirted ten jets of formic acid so accurately that a crystal drop of the poison immediately formed upon the end of the blade.

I feel sure that insects have a very high degree of intelligence, or perhaps I should say that insects are very highly gifted.   For instance, I know a man who had a chrysalis from which there emerged a female moth.   He placed it in a box upon his desk and within an hour there were about twenty male moths fluttering around it, and the nearest place from which the moths could have come was about a mile from the house.

I know of another instance in which a male cricket was placed inside a box which was purposely provided with a tightly fitting lid.   It could not see out of the box.   It remained quiet and unconcerned until a female cricket, also imprisoned in a similar box, was brought into the room, and then, although no sound of any kind could be heard, the male cricket was apparently aware of the presence of the female and was in communication with her.

As we made our way up the river, the country rapidly became wilder and the people also.   Children, as soon as they saw my face, would run screaming up the river banks.

One day while I was lying in my boat, which was being poled up the Tanum, I heard a shot and, looking up, I saw a little boy jump from a tree into the river. He swam like a dog. He had been shooting fish. He sat up in the tree, throwing bait into the water, and, when a fish came to the surface, he fired.

I landed and looked at his gun and found marked upon the barrel these words: "The Tower of London, 1800." The bullets were as big as marbles. The boy was a funny youngster about nine years old—a typical little naked *orang ulu*. He had a shaved skull, except for an absurd tuft of hair, about a foot long, which denoted that he had not yet been initiated into Islam. His name was Isa, or Jesus.

When Isa found I could speak Malay, he took me to his village and produced a bottle. Much to my disappointment, it contained a fish. Then a friend of his, called Noh—that is, Noah—came along with another bottle that had a fish inside, and they placed their bottles on a table. The fish were about two inches long—rather ugly and ordinary-looking. Isa and Noh immediately began to discuss them and to talk about their good points. Isa's fish was the hero of no less than forty fights and had several scars on its little body. Noh's fish was larger than Isa's but did not look quite so intelligent! The two bottles were now placed side by side, and, as soon as they touched, the little fish glowed with gorgeous colours and began biting at each other through the glass. By this time a crowd had gathered, shouting and betting, and as soon as the bets were made a referee poured the water from one bottle into the other. The fish fought until you could scarcely see them for the scales that floated about.

"*Itu dîa, sudah luka!* [That's the way! He is wounded!]" yelled Isa.

"*Dîa lari!* [He is running away!]"

"*Mampus!* [He has kicked the bucket!]" shrieked Isa, as Noh's fish sank to the bottom of the bottle, dead.

That story sounds "fishy," but fish-fighting is a national pastime in Malaya, just as fishing is an everyday occupation. That afternoon Noh took me with him when he went fishing in his father's rice-field. It was almost harvest-time and the rice was nearly as tall as the boy. Instead of one good-sized rod, he carried no less than twenty little rods, each about two feet long, and he stuck them all over the field, leaving the hooks dangling in the water in which the rice was growing. When he had set all the rods, he went back to the first one, took off a fish about three inches long, and put it into a basket. He then went from rod to rod until he had caught about a hundred fish. He was ready to start home but, just to amuse himself, he picked out one of the fish and rubbed it on the ground. The fish began to get fat, it swallowed air in big gulps and, as its body swelled, it grew round and tight like a ball. Then Noh whacked it on the ground. It bounced up into the air, fell back into the water, squirted the air out, and swam away—a perfectly sound Malay puffing-fish. It was new to me then, but afterward it became familiar enough. I have seen Malay boys with several fish blown up tight prick them with a knife to hear them pop, but those did not swim again.

I left Isa and Noh regretfully and returned to my boat. Soon we were so far upstream that we ran on the bottom of the river. The coolies then got out and built a lock. Sometimes after that they built locks two or three times a day to enable the boats to go on up the shallow stream. When we came to a waterfall, four or five feet high, perhaps, the coolies would make an immense rope out of jungle vines and then drag the boats over the fall. One of the most amusing sights that my eyes took in during our slow progress up the river was a lot of monkeys that came down out of a tree at about sunset and waded into the water to wash their teeth.

One evening, just before sunset, I saw at least fifty monkeys fishing in the river; some were standing on rocks and others were in the water up to their waists.

I saw one big monkey bend down and lift up a rock while the others put their hands underneath the rock and caught little fish which they ate. In fact, on the east coast of the Malay Peninsula there is a certain kind of monkey that lives almost entirely upon crabs.

After three weeks of "bucking" the Tanum, we came to a tributary about twelve feet wide up which we turned. About every hundred yards we had to get out of the boats and drag them through the shallows.

Eventually we got so far upstream that we could not go on in the boats; so we abandoned them and entered the jungle. That day, when I was walking along an old elephant track, I came to a little bush about a foot high, covered with red flowers. I thought I would have a boutonnière; so I picked a flower. As soon as I touched the bush, its leaves closed up, its branches folded themselves, and it lay down. I waited quietly and watched it as it slowly and cautiously came to life again. I blew at it, and although it was used to real wind, it recognized the artificial breeze and at once lay down flat. It was a mimosa, or sensitive plant. Later, I saw large areas of it lie down when a buffalo began to eat one edge. It is very convenient on a golf course because you never lose a ball; you see, if the ball goes into the rough, one of the bushes lies down!

I shall never forget the first time I had a drink of

water in the jungle.   I used to drink hot malted milk as a rule, but one day my servant forgot to bring the thermos flask, and I was expressing my appreciation of the fact when the Malay walked over to a tree and cut down a piece of wood about three feet long and three inches thick.

Apparently it was solid, yet I noticed that he carried it very carefully, with both ends the same height.   Then, beckoning me to open my mouth, he tipped up one end of the wood and gave me a long drink of deliciously cold water out of the other.

Taking my knife, I went over to the same tree and cut another piece of wood, but it was absolutely dry!

"What is the matter with it?"   I exclaimed.

"Oh!" said the Malay, "you made too much noise; it knew you were coming!"

The next time I saw one of those trees I surprised it successfully.   The same day that we abandoned the boats, we reached Mat Noh's first camp.   It consisted of an open space cleared in the very heart of the jungle, and in the middle of the space were two little Malay houses.

The first thing I did was to go up the steps and examine the roof.   There were the usual lizards, of course, but something darted out of the roof and caught a lizard.   It was a snake.   I found that the roof of my house was full of lizards and snakes, scorpions and rats, mice, centipedes, frogs, spiders, cockroaches and other things. It was simply because the roof was made of the leaf of the *nipa* palm, which cockroaches live upon. So the roaches went up to eat the roof; then the lizards went up to eat the roaches; then something else went up to eat the lizards; last of all the snakes went up to eat everything. So I did what every engineer in Malaya does: I pitched a tent inside my house.

Still I was beset by creatures that creep and fly. As I sat at my table, drawing a plan, something dropped on my head and things began crawling over my neck. I brushed them off and found that my fingers were covered with tiny white spiders. Above me a spider as big as a saucer was walking along. She had attached to her a kind of soup plate in which she was carrying her babies; but she had tripped over something and I got the soup. A little later, when I was resting in a long chair, I heard a noise like this: "Whoo, whoo, whoo, whoo, ha, ha, ha, ha!" I called one of my servants and asked, "What on earth made that noise?" "It was only a bird, sir," he answered. But what a bird! I thought when I saw it. It was about five feet long from one end to the other, and it had short legs and black and white feathers and a beak about a foot long with a huge casque on top. It was blessed with the name of "hornbill."

There are many kinds of hornbills, in both Africa and Asia, varying from about the size of a pigeon to the huge bird I have described. Most of them rarely descend to the ground and have very short legs, but there is one variety that spends most of its time on the ground and is therefore provided with very long legs. All the hornbills have long beaks and a peculiar horny growth called a casque on the top of the head. In one Malayan variety the casque is much prized for use in jewellery.

In the course of time I grew familiar with the squawks of the Malayan tree hornbill and I could tell the sound of his great wings quite a mile away. The Malays called him the feathered oddity. Though his beak is huge, his tongue is tiny. So he is compelled to feed by throwing his food from the tip of his beak into the air, sometimes as high as five or six feet, and letting it fall into his wide-open mouth and drop down his throat. In some respects his diet is curious. He thrives, for instance, upon strychnine, and during the nesting season he feeds it in huge quantities to his wife, whom he has put inside a large hollow tree and plastered in with mud. He has left a hole about five inches in diameter through which she can stick her beak, and there she sits, moulting, for two and a half months. Her wings and her tail

Compare this Sakai family with the Semang in the frontispiece, and the difference in type will at once be apparent.

and all her feathers drop out.   When her one or two little birds have hatched and have grown to be about as big as ducks, they help the old bird out of the tree by breaking down the mud wall, and they all come out fat and healthy because they have been fed all the time by the male hornbill.   Of course, he does not spend the whole day near his family and let everyone see where his nest is.   But he visits it every two or three days.   Also it happens that at this time of year the lining of his crop comes loose.   So he goes off into the jungle, has a feast, comes back to the nest, brings up his crop lining full of fruit, and hands it to his wife!   During certain seasons of the year, I understand that the hornbill in the New York Zoo periodically brings up the lining of his crop and, of course, gets a new one.

That the Malayan hornbill should thrive upon what to us would be deadly poison is not so remarkable as it sounds.   Only a short time ago I heard of an instance in which a number of small animals had been found inside a packet of cocaine upon which they were not only feeding entirely but also increasing; in fact, they had large families.

It was nearly sunset and the jungle was resounding with the screeches and toots of strange insects when Salleh came up to me and said:

"I am sorry, sir, but I can't sleep in the house you have built for me. You have put it so close to the jungle that I can hear things."

As a matter of fact, I had been hearing things all day myself, and I must admit that I felt distinctly jumpy at the prospect of sleeping for the first time in my life in the real jungle, far from civilization, especially now that Salleh wanted to leave me alone. I remembered that I had a revolver. It was an Ivor Johnson, and it always shot straight up into the air, no matter what I did to it. But I tapped my belt and said: "If you are frightened, you may go to sleep with the coolies." So off he went and left me alone.

As soon as it was dark, I lighted my lamp and began to read. When I had just got myself pleasantly settled, a tree fell down. I jumped a bit; for the tree was so covered with vines and creepers that, as it fell, it carried about a dozen trees with it and for several seconds the noise was like thunder. After it had died away, I could hear nothing for about half an hour except the yelling of monkeys. They must have been sleeping in the tree-tops and been suddenly thrown out of bed. The crash had so unsettled my nerves that I thought: "Heavens! what is going to happen next?"

I did not have long to wait, because I had just recovered myself and was in the middle of a very exciting story and it was absolutely dark and still when I heard a muffled "Ho, ho, ho!"

My hair stuck straight up into the air and I thought to myself: "Good Lord, what was that?"

Then I heard it again—"Ho, ho, ho!" So I got hold of an electric flashlight and went all over the house, trying to find the source of the noise. Next I heard it outside the house. So I crept down the steps and came to a big rock. The noise was coming out of the rock. Soon I found a large hole and there at the bottom of the hole sat a frog as big as a coconut, with his open mouth uttering those hair-raising croaks. I was so relieved that I went back into the house in good spirits, got into bed, with the lamp on a table beside me, tucked the mosquito net all around the mattress, and was soon lost in my story. Then something began to squeak up in the roof, the leaves rustled about, an object fell on top of the tent and slithered down the canvas to the ground with a flop, and I saw a snake swallowing a rat. When everything was quiet once more, it was really time for me to turn in. Just to be on the safe side, I put underneath my head a box of matches and my revolver.

About two hours afterward I woke with a start. There was something in my bedroom. I strained my eyes through the darkness and tried in vain to find the matches. Then I lay perfectly still, perspiring violently. Suddenly, close by my bed, about two feet from the ground, I saw, glowing and gleaming, two great green eyes. "Heavens!" I thought, "it's a tiger!" I got hold of my revolver, which was wabbling like a jelly, aimed at the eyes, shot with a bang right through the mosquito net and set it on fire. Then, by the light of the burning net I discovered that I had shot at my cat—but had not hit her. She had been sitting on my suitcase beside the bed, and I, knowing that my revolver always shot up into the air, had aimed specially low, fired right through the suitcase and spoiled all my clothes. I was so angry that, as I got back into bed with a piece of string and tied up the hole in the mosquito net, I said to myself: "I won't get up again to-night, even for an elephant!"

One of our boats. It would carry three more men quite easily.

CHAPTER IX

I CERTAINLY shall never forget those first few weeks in the jungle when I was as green as the foliage around me. Like most other people, my idea of a jungle was that it was a place swarming with tigers and elephants, and until I became used to the solitude and the strange noises, I was always having the most exciting experiences, chiefly caused by my own state of mind.

One of the most important parts of a camp was always the bathroom! Every time I went in something crawled out, and as soon as I began taking a bath I was immediately joined by a colony of fat frogs. When Mat Noh constructed my camps, he never seemed able to put the bathroom in the same place twice running, a habit of his which led to strange results.

One evening I reached a new camp at nightfall, tired out, and went straight to bed. At about midnight, something awakened me, and as I lay there I heard a noise like a trumpet, then another and another. Every now and then I could hear a branch being torn down and I realized that there were elephants all around the house. Seizing my shotgun, which was loaded with fine snipeshot, I rushed outside and there, right in front of me, was a big black thing, and with a bang that roused the whole camp, I shot it! But it didn't move and I discovered I had shot the bathroom!

The only time I ever actually shot an elephant was one morning when we came across five of them feeding on *rotan* in a swamp. Mr. Carl Akeley will no doubt wonder how my mind works when I state that I deliberately stalked those elephants and shot one five times with my Ivor Johnson revolver, but the animal didn't seem to mind much. I know I hit it, but the elephant simply gave a peculiar little squeal and with its companions floundered out of the swamps and disappeared into the jungle.

I had a most interesting experience that lasted for five years in connection with an elephant that the Malays called Gaja Kramat. The first time I saw his tracks they were carefully pointed out to me by Hussein, who showed me that the elephant was deformed because one of his hind feet was only about half as large as the other. This happened in 1914, close to my camp at Kuala Tanum. The next time I saw those tracks, which were unmistakable, was in Siam on the banks of the Golo River in 1915. The third time was in Kedah in 1918, in a rubber estate, and the manager of the estate told me that early one morning he had seen an elephant with a deformed hind leg walking from tree to tree taking the china cups that were hanging on the rubber trees to collect the latex and throwing them on the ground. The same elephant, which was undoubtedly Gaja Kramat, the same day walked down to the landing place on the river bank in this estate, untied a boat, and let it float away down the river. In fact, Gaja Kramat was well known all over the Malay Peninsula and evidently was not hindered by his deformity from travelling hundreds of miles and crossing the main mountain ranges. Kramat is still alive, and will probably die a natural death (that is to say, if elephants ever do die a natural death) because no one would ever think of killing him.

My life in camp was very much enlivened by the adventures of Adam and Eve. Originally I had intended the turkeys for my Christmas and New Year's dinners, and when I took them into the jungle I was told that they would die long before then without grass to eat, but they actually thrived upon a diet of rice and insects! They spent their time foraging in the jungle, only appearing in camp at the roll call in the morning and whenever they heard me shout:

"Boy, *bawa makanan!* [Boy, bring food!]" Then they appeared promptly, and Adam would immediately spread his tail and start strutting.

One day we missed Eve, and after great search discovered a nest with eight eggs in it, but, alas! No Eve. The ground about the nest showed the imprints of a tiger's paw, and I was so upset at losing my pet turkey that I called a council of war and announced two days' holiday and a tiger hunt!

The Malays set to work eagerly and constructed an enormous trap like an old-fashioned mousetrap, with a door. The trap and door were made of heavy logs and weighed about a ton, while at the back of it was a small cage in which we placed several chickens.

About midnight, just when the whole camp was asleep and everything was still, the chickens began squawking. In a few minutes the place was in an uproar; lights were flashing, men shouting, and Salleh rushed in to me shouting: "*Tûan! Limau!* [Sir! Lemon!]" Of course, he meant to say: "*Rimau,*" which means "tiger." As I hastily pulled on a pair of trousers, I could hear the frantic shrieking of the chickens and the snarls of the imprisoned animal. We had two guns in camp and a revolver besides numerous spears and dozens of knives. With my usual politeness I allowed the cook to lead the way in the darkness, carrying a torch in one hand and a large meat chopper in the other, while I followed with an ordinary shotgun (12 bore) and an excited mob of Malays bringing up the rear with parangs and spears.

All the time I was wondering how on earth we were going to get the animal out of the trap and kill it now that we had caught it. Eventually we reached the trap, and from it came the most unearthly mixture of chicken-squawking and fierce growls. It was impossible to see what was going on inside, because the Malays in constructing the trap had carefully avoided leaving the least crack or hole through which a tiger might thrust his paw and break out. Then one of these rare flashes of genius came to my rescue. Why not bore several holes in the trap, fit our gun barrels into them, and shoot the animal within?

Salleh caught on to the idea at once and rushed off to get an auger. Every time he approached the trap the noise increased so much and the trap rocked so violently that the poor old cook turned perfectly green with fright. So, impatiently snatching up the auger, I successfully bored six holes, about an inch in diameter. It took but a moment to thrust our gun barrels into the holes and pour a regular fusillade in the trap. Soon all was silent, but as a precaution we all loaded up again and with our guns and spears surrounded the trap while four men slowly levered it open, and there, stretched out in a pool of blood and chickens was an animal like a weasel, about two feet long.

I looked at Salleh and Salleh looked at me! He was right, after all. I had caught a lemon.

After the untimely death of Eve, Adam became so miserable that I sent him away to lead a happier life in his old home, as I never could have had the heart to eat him.

Christmas came soon after Adam left me, and although I was the only Christian for miles, I celebrated the festival in every possible way I could think of. The day happened to be fearfully hot, and while the coolies decorated the house with evergreens and large imitation poinsettias, I sang "While Shepherds Watched Their Flocks by Night." Salleh, although he was a Mohammedan, was still sufficiently Chinese to be perfectly delighted when I opened a case of fire crackers, and he spent most of his time setting them off in all kinds of queer places, firmly believing that I had purchased the crackers for the purpose of driving away ghosts and evil spirits.

This was my first Christmas away from home, and I was determined to have a real Christmas dinner. Unfortunately, in the absence of Adam, I had to put up with a full-grown roast deer which was served up whole on my dinner plate! The Christmas pudding, however, was to be the *pièce de résistance!* Six weeks

previously I had ordered from Singapore all the necessary ingredients for one, including suet, raisins,
candied peel, almonds, and the numerous other items
that go to make that most famous of all puddings,
Christmas Pudding. Salleh took the keenest interest in preparing everything, although he hadn't
the faintest idea what on earth I was going to do with
such an extraordinary mixture, and when finally I
told him that the pudding was to be boiled for eight
hours, he nearly collapsed at the prospect of cutting
up so much firewood. The largest boiler I could
find was the big iron kettle that was used for heating
my bath water. So that was pressed into service.
Dinner was served at two o'clock as I sat in solitude
amid the most magnificent decorations I ever saw in
my life for a Christmas dinner. In one corner was a
Christmas tree and on the top of it were two unopened
letters, one from my mother and the other from my
wife. Beside me sat the black cat, while Rose of
Sharon and Sahar, looking absurdly alike, watched
me in amazement from the veranda. Outside I
could see the heads of the coolies peeping at me with
the greatest curiosity.

After eating the whole deer, I called for the Christmas pudding and in walked Salleh, looking very much
puzzled, carrying a large soup plate in one hand and
a huge black kettle in the other. Before I could re-

cover from my astonishment he had placed the plate before me and was solemnly pouring the pudding out of the spout! Then it dawned upon me that I had forgotten to tell him anything about tying up the pudding in a cloth before boiling it! Realizing that the fault was mine, with praiseworthy control I ordered him to bring in a canned Christmas pudding which I had purchased in case of accidents, and re moved the "soup." The little canned pudding was then placed in a dish and served in a blaze of blue flames of burning brandy. Finally I pulled a Tom Smith's bonbon cracker and crowned myself with a tall paper hat and began to feel horribly homesick.

As I recall these incidents and their sequence, the buying of the turkey and eating a deer instead, the tedious preparation of a Christmas pudding and then eating instead a burning canned one, the tying of the two letters to the top of a tree instead of opening them, and finally making myself look absurd in a paper hat, I am not in the least surprised that Sahar and everyone else thought I was perfectly crazy, nor can I wonder that they took the greatest interest in watching the strange rites that I performed that day, especially when I finished up the evening by eating snapdragon. I can still hear the coolies' shrieks of delight as I popped into my mouth the blazing raisins.

A few days after Christmas the weather seemed to

Evening dress!　A sarong and singlet.

break up and almost every day there was a terrific thunderstorm accompanied by torrential rains. The jungle became absolutely waterlogged, but the rain always came at the same time, namely, about one o'clock, so that I was usually able to put in a good morning's work before it arrived, although often I was caught in the rain as I returned to camp. The country had become extremely hilly and there were numerous lovely waterfalls and rushing mountain torrents instead of rivers. I saw the fresh tracks of elephant, rhinoceros, tiger, and tapir every day, and occasionally those of the seladang, that magnificent wild bull, the ancestor of our domestic cattle.

It surprised me that I rarely saw any animals except a few monkeys, and although the jungle was full of birds of all sizes, from the tiniest to enormous ones like the hornbill, the Argus pheasant, and the peacock, and I heard their calls continually, I scarcely ever saw one. I did have one very narrow escape from being attacked by a wild boar. The incident occurred one day as I was returning to camp by myself in the middle of a thunderstorm, when I suddenly walked into about a dozen wild pigs.

They were striped, almost like a tiger, and were busily engaged in rooting about in the rain when I came upon them The noise of the rain had prevented them hearing my approach, but when they saw me they stampeded wildly and the big boar turned round and rushed by me, missing my leg by about an inch.

I remember telling my experience to a friend of mine in Kedah called Parker, whose experience with a wild boar had not been so lucky. He was walking through his rubber estate one morning and saw a large pig on the other side of a ravine tearing the bark off one of the young rubber trees. Thinking he would frighten the animal away, he shouted and struck his cane against a tree, making a loud crack like a rifle shot. The boar looked up and then to the dismay of Parker rushed down the side of the hill, crossed the ravine, climbed up to where he stood, and savagely attacked him. The animal rushed between Parker's legs and, as it passed, deeply gashed both legs with its tusks. The boar then did it again and was about to do it for the third time when Parker, with his trousers torn to pieces and very seriously injured, lay down and rolled himself to the bottom of the ravine—an undignified performance which undoubtedly saved his life. As it was, he spent weeks in the hospital, and when he came out there were five or six long deep scars on the inside of his legs, in between his knees and his thighs.

I am quite sure that the best time to see animals in the jungle is during a rainstorm, because otherwise their keen sense of hearing warns them. One day I was walking back to the same camp when I heard the unmistakable noise of rain in the distance. It grew louder and louder until, with a roar like thunder, the rain arrived. The jungle was so dense that the rain did not penetrate directly to the ground but rushed down the trunks of the trees and poured in streams down every branch. I was wet through almost immediately and as I tramped along with the rain beating on the leaves like the noise of a waterfall, I saw walking in front of me two little bears about fifteen inches high. They were not cubs but the ordinary honey bear or *bruang* of Malay.

Quickly I hid myself and watched them as they sniffed around, looking for something to eat. Suddenly, they both looked up in the air, and when I followed their gaze I could see hanging from the branch of the tree a honeycomb about three feet long. One of the bears commenced to climb the tree but when he was about ten feet from the ground he got stuck! So his wife climbed up underneath him and gave him a bump up! And up they went, bump! bump! bump! I happened to be carrying in my hand a small shot 22 bore rifle, and when they were about twenty feet from the ground I carefully aimed at the bear on top, but I purposely aimed at the fur on his back in order not to injure him. The noise of the rain prevented the bear from hearing the faint report of the 22. And when the bullet skimmed through the fur of his hind quarters he was the most surprised bear in the world. He looked around for a second or two and then knocked his wife off the tree, scrambled down, and smacked her face! He thought she had spitefully scratched his back. Then they noticed me and as they hurried away into the undergrowth I could not help thinking how often such unjust punishments occur in our own lives, and I felt very sorry for the faithful wife.

One morning, just as I was about to go to work, Mat Noh, the old man who was building my camps ahead of me, arrived in camp. He had come to receive the first payment on his contract and I was filled with excitement when he reported that we were in the very heart of the district from which he recruited his jungle men. We were, in fact, only a few miles from the base of Gunong Tahan, the Forbidden Mountain.

Yorkshire had told me that I would never see any of the really wild *Semang* or Negrito dwarfs because he had tried unsuccessfully to do so for the last ten years. But I knew that if ever I was going to get a glimpse of the lowest form of human being in the world I should never have a better chance than now. I therefore commenced taking my camera out to work

The use of cosmetics is common among these aboriginal Sakai. This picture clearly shows the result of various intermarriages.

with me daily.   Mat Noh told me that he had about nine *Semang* cutting down trees and collecting *rotan* but that he saw them only occasionally and even then they usually ran away, although they knew they were working for him.   I learned from Mat Noh that he and his two Malay companions worked as follows: First they selected a camp site and felled the trees in a rough square where the houses were to be built. They then went ahead to the next camp site, and while they were at work there, the *Semang* left their supplies of jungle poles and *rotan* in the first empty space.   Here I thought was an opportunity of seeing the dwarfs, because I planned to surprise them at work one day and secure some coveted photographs.

The scheme did not work, however, because no matter how careful I was or how long I lay concealed watching the camp site that was intended for my future use there was never a sign of a dwarf.   I would return at frequent intervals to find the place deserted but always a bigger pile of *rotan* and logs.   Then it was that I realized that I myself was being watched by the Negritos.   Sometimes I would discover where these little people had slept—just a lair on the ground with the branches twisted to form a rude protection from the dew.   And I was very excited when I discovered a large fireplace, still warm.   It was a fresh sleeping place of the Negritos, who have a habit of sleeping in their fireplaces covered with ashes in order to keep warm at night! It was quite evident that we had certainly reached the district where there were plenty of jungle men, because several times that day we came across places where they had been digging up the ground in search of edible roots.

I had almost given up hope that I would ever see a really wild man, especially as Yorkshire, who had spent fifteen years in the jungle, had never seen any except those semi-savage ones that are sometimes seen around villages and who pose for their photographs for scientists. But one day, after getting tired of watching the camp site, I started home, and just as I was walking down the new cutting that we had surveyed that morning, a little mouse deer darted like an arrow across my path. Of course, I hadn't a chance to take a photograph of it, but just for sport I thought I would try to attract the deer's attention in the way that I had seen Hussein do, by means of a leaf and two sticks. In a few minutes I had made a very respectable blind, and crawling inside with my camera I began drumming on a leaf, doing my best to imitate the mouse deer's challenge. My camera was in readiness to snap the animal, when suddenly, without any warning and without the slightest noise, a little man walked into the clearing. He was naked except for a little piece of bark and stood with his mouth open looking around him in a puzzled manner.

I think he had heard a noise and had been deceived by it, or else he thought another dwarf was doing it. Pausing for a moment, he made a peculiar noise and within ten seconds, in a most astonishing manner considering the thickness of the jungle, two women appeared carrying two babies in slings across their bodies. The man was not so heavily built as were the women, but none of them was more than four feet six inches in height. The women also were naked except for a diminutive apron made of bark. They had thick lips, woolly hair, and were of a blackish gray colour. Every now and then the women would jerk the babies up in their slings in order to get them in a more comfortable position, and the poor little babies would pucker up their faces in agony and the tears roll down, because they were covered with jungle sores. The most surprising thing of all was that the babies never uttered a sound and I could only conclude that they had been trained to cry silently. It was several seconds before I recovered myself sufficiently to take a photograph. The shutter gave a click. The man started and looked straight into the camera. Then one of the women looked behind her and as silently as they had appeared the whole family disappeared, gliding with extraordinary speed and silence into the jungle. That night when the negative was developed I discovered to my joy that with the exception of the man's right hand I had succeeded in photographing the whole group, in spite of being unable to wait in order to use the view finder for fear of losing the picture altogether.

CHAPTER X

MY MOSQUITO boots lasted nearly a year from the time I left London, and it was when I was camped in the mountains, almost upon the boundary of Pahang and Kelantan, that I discarded them.

Two or three weeks afterward I came home from work suffering with a headache; soon I began shivering and my skin became like gooseskin. Recognizing that these were the symptoms that Yorkshire always had when an attack of malaria was coming, I at once followed his advice, took fifteen grains of aspirin and rolled up in a blanket. Although it was an extremely hot day I simply froze and shivered until my teeth chattered. Half an hour afterward I became so hot that I longed to fling off the blanket, but I kept it on and within an hour I began to perspire so profusely that if I shut my eyes my eye socket filled with water and overflowed down my face. My hair became soaking wet and soon I was literally lying in a bath of perspiration which soaked clean through the mattress. When the perspiration ceased I took twenty grains of quinine and it was not long before my ears began to sing. The attack had come on at 2 o'clock, but at 5 o'clock my temperature had dropped from 102 to below normal, and except for being as weak as a kitten, I felt quite well. The next day I went to work as usual, but a few days afterward I had another attack. After three attacks of fever in a month, I decided to leave camp and go down the river to Kuala Lipis, so one morning we cut through the jungle and reached a small stream that was running into the Tanum River where we built a bamboo raft. All day we alternately floated downstream or shot the rapids until late in the evening, when we reached our boats where we had concealed them on the river bank.

Since I had only two Malay coolies with me we took the smallest boat and started down the river. The second day, just as we were passing a small island, I heard my name called and, looking up, I was surprised to recognize Siti! There she was, sitting on the beach with a small bundle of clothes and her accordion beside her, marooned upon this tiny island in the wildest part of the jungle. When I asked her what was the matter she explained: "*Tûan, Yorkshire suda buang!* [Master, Yorkshire has got rid of me!]"

I then asked her what she intended doing about it, and she replied: "*Tiada apa!* [nothing!]" I left the fair maiden on the island. She stayed there all night but I afterward heard that she was rescued by some Malays the next day and returned to Yorkshire who reinstated her.

The journey that had taken about three weeks to accomplish going upstream took only about three days going downstream, and when I reached Kuala Lipis I went straight to the hospital and stayed there a week. As I was the only patient I had the sole attention of the doctor and the nurse. Franklin, the District Officer, came every day with delicacies and prayer, the combination being so successful that at the end of the week I took part in a football match between government officials and the local Malay football team. The game was soccer, and while we white men all played in football boots, the Malays played barefoot. It was perfectly astonishing to watch them kicking that football with the bare toes. The match attracted a large crowd of natives besides dozens of pariah dogs which took the keenest interest in the game until there resounded through the field a loud thud. To my dismay, that thud, which was meaningless to me, had a most extraordinary effect upon everyone else, because the football game stopped and players, spectators, and dogs dashed off into the bushes and began hunting about for something. Suddenly there was a shout as a dreadful looking dog emerged from the undergrowth chased by a crowd of natives. The animal was carrying in its mouth a large green fruit about the size of a coconut and covered with large spikes.

It was a durian!

I shall never forget this first experience with a durian because I argued that if the sound of one falling off a tree could completely stop a football match and cause every person and animal in the neighbourhood to look for it, there must be some strong attraction. However, as the dog had secured this one, the football match was resumed. I spoke to Franklin about it and he promised me one for breakfast the next morning.

The durian grows upon a large tree, often eighty or a hundred feet high, and the fruit can usually be seen plainly hanging upon the branches away up high on the tree-top. In fact, the durians can easily be counted. They vary considerably in size, shape, and flavour on different trees and in different localities. Some are round and about five inches in diameter; others are oval and about twice as large. The durians are covered with large pyramid-like spikes which the Malays explain were put there by God for their special benefit. The reason they give is very ingenious. Durians are not supposed to be fit to eat unless they actually drop off the tree, which they do at very uncertain and irregular intervals. As the fruit is much sought after, not only by human beings but also by all animals, including even tigers, there is always a mixed crowd in the neighbourhood of any durian tree when the fruit is ripening.

In order, therefore, to keep away animals, Malays usually build a strong fence around the tree, within which they build a little house where they idle, sleep, and pray, until they hear the unmistakable thud of a ripe durian dropping. They then rush out and find the fruit, and either eat it at once or store it for a feast or to sell in the market. Unfortunately, it sometimes happens that a ripe durian drops on top of a Malay, and as the fruit often weighs five or six pounds it is no pleasant experience to be hit by one falling from a height, say, of eighty feet. If the fruit were smooth and round, the Malays say that the blow would cause a severe bruise from which death might result, so to prevent this, God placed spikes on the durian so that they would puncture the skin, let the blood flow, and thus, instead of inflicting a dangerous bruise, cause only a scratch or a cut.

When the fruit is opened it is found to contain about eight or nine large seeds about the size of a chestnut which are covered with a thick, custard-like substance. It is a very messy business eating a durian, because the seeds are taken in the fingers and the custard is then sucked off, resulting in a custardy face.

A durian tastes like a mixture of sweet custard, turpentine, and rotten onions, and it smells like a sewer. The first time I tried to eat one I was almost sick, but one day I determined to eat a durian even if I died in the attempt, and I was so successful that I ate three.

Franklin's breakfast was no attraction for me because the smell nearly knocked me down long before I saw the fruit, but in after years I attended many durian breakfasts. Nothing is eaten except huge quantities of durians washed down with copious draughts of neat brandy, which gives you strength to continue. And I must admit that nothing is more delicious than a durian breakfast.

The day after the football match I motored from Kuala Lipis to a health station in the main range of the mountains, called The Gap. As we climbed the jungle-covered mountains it became cooler and cooler and sometimes I felt a delicious gust of really cold air rushing down some mountain ravine. After a few hours' journey we arrived at a lovely bungalow covered with pink roses set in the very midst of a beautiful rose garden and surrounded by jungle-covered hills on every side. As I entered the house a cloud enveloped us, and for several minutes there was a dense mist. The house was in charge of two Chinese servants, but there were no other people there. The temperature that night dropped to about 60 degrees F. and it felt like winter as I warmed myself in front of a blazing fire. The beds had thick blankets and sheets, and Dutch wives were quite unnecessary.

Up here I noticed several trees that were not to be seen in the low-lying jungle, especially several varieties of tree ferns. One evening I heard a great commotion in the fowl house and we caught a *musang*, which I recognized as the kind of animal that I had once before caught in my tiger trap. This particular *musang* had been stealing the cook's chickens, he told me, every night for a week, and this was the punishment meted out to the wretched beast! The two Chinamen carefully sewed up the *musang's* mouth with cobbler's thread and then released him to starve to death.

I had been at the Gap only a few days when I received orders to proceed to the State of Kelantan and take charge of the construction of the railway there. I spent the next month in returning to my camp, handing over my work to Yorkshire, once again shooting the rapids of the Tanum and then down the Jelei and back to my starting point at Tembeling.

Here I took the train back to Seremban, accompanied by Sahar, Salleh, and Hussein. My old cat I left with Siti, to whom I also presented, much to her delight, Samson, a fighting cock that I had acquired. Rose of Sharon, alas, had met with a violent death.

CHAPTER XI

I ARRIVED in Seremban on Whitsunday and decided to call on the Church of England padre, Mr. Danson. When I entered his bungalow I found the padre surrounded by medicine bottles and hot drinks, suffering from a severe cold. He had cancelled all church services, but when he heard I had come straight from the jungle, after being in it for a year, and that I was on my way to Kelantan, he decided to hold a special service for my benefit! So that Whitsunday will ever remain in my memory although the congregation consisted of only the sexton and me. Mr. Danson, who is now Bishop Danson, held a full festival service, including a short address, so that I left for Kelantan strengthened not only physically but also spiritually.

When we arrived in Singapore I found that there would be two days to wait before the next boat for Kelantan. Sahar, Salleh, and Hussein immediately borrowed a month's wages in advance and I did not see them again until the morning the ship sailed, when Sahar and Hussein, the two Malays, arrived stony-broke, but Salleh, the Chinaman, reported that he had won sixty dollars gambling in Johore Bharu, the Malay town just opposite Singapore upon the mainland.

Gambling and the sale of opium were government monopolies in certain parts of the Malay Peninsula. The right to gamble was "farmed" or sold periodically to certain rich Chinamen who paid the Government an enormous sun of money in return for the sole right to operate gambling houses. Opium is sold under government control and its quality is therefore guaranteed.

The most popular gambling game is called *main po* and is played with a single die which is similar to ordinary dice but is coloured half red and half white on each face. This red-and-white die fits closely inside a brass cube which in turn fits into another heavy brass cube. The brass cube containing the smaller one and the die is placed at the centre of a table about four feet square, the top of which is divided into four triangles by means of two diagonal lines. The triangles are numbered from one to four, and the brass cube containing the die is placed at the intersection of the two diagonals. Money is placed on the numbers and any gambler has the right to spin around the brass cube. He lifts the cube slowly allowing the smaller one inside to slip out and expose the red-and-white die. The winning number is the one opposite to the red on the die, and the odds are three to one. Ten per cent. of all winnings is retained by the bank.

We sailed from Singapore on a little white steamer called the *Sapho*. The captain was a Dane, and there was only one other passenger besides myself, who was a diamond merchant on his way to sell jewels to the Sultan of Kelantan. The merchant had a German name, but he said he was a Swiss. Two days after leaving Singapore we anchored outside the surf off the Coast of Kelantan at the mouth of the Kelantan River.

The journey up the East Coast was entirely different from the journey between Penang and Singapore down the West Coast. Here on the East, instead of dismal mangrove swamps and mud flats, were lovely stretches of pure white sand fringed with coconut palms and beautiful casuarina trees. Sea-snakes were common. We landed at Tumpat and there I found a private car awaiting me which was hitched on to the end of a construction train, and after four hours I arrived at my destination, the railhead at a tiny village called Tana Merah. Tana Merah means red earth, and the soil was very much the colour of that in Devonshire.

Evidently my arrival had been expected, because no sooner did I leave the train than I was escorted to a large shed where, sitting at a table, was a white man. Before him were about twelve bottles of champagne and several bottles of whisky, while the ground around him was carpeted with cases of beer. Encircling the shed was a crowd of natives, while here and there was one obviously prosperous and either a Chinaman or a Sikh, a Tamil or an Afghan. These were the contractors and they had come to welcome me and say good-bye to the man whom I was succeeding.

After we two engineers had partaken of a modest amount of champagne, the crowd partook of the remainder and all work ceased for the day. The man I was relieving was also a "Swiss," although he had a German name, and it seemed queer to have met two "Swiss" in so short a time.

After he had left Kelantan on the *Sapho* I settled down to my first construction job in the country. My monthly expenditure in payment of contractors and coolie wages was sometimes as much as twenty thousand dollars, and I soon discovered that I was surrounded by the biggest crowd of rogues that walked the face of the earth. Even my chief clerk used to charge two dollars admission for any one who desired an interview with me. His name was Lyman, and he was a Jafna Tamil and a Christian. His salary was one hundred dollars a month with a

Aboriginal Sakai hunting with the "sumpit" or blow pipe and poisoned dart. One of the jungle's silent deaths.

furnished house, and he was tall, thin, and as black as the ace of spades.   Every morning he would place upon my desk a list of appointments for the day; usually he would have about eight contractors on the list who desired an interview.   Each one had to pay Lyman two dollars for the privilege!   When I discovered his game I fired him and I afterward learned that he had joined a political society called the Friends of Freedom for India, which I believe has offices in Washington.

We had a great deal of trouble with constructing the railway in Kelantan because the Malays objected strongly to the "right of way."   Soon after I took up my duty there, the chief engineer, Mr. Openshaw, came on a visit of inspection and I met him at Tumpat with an engine and a private car. On our way home to Tana Merah, while we were bowling along merrily at thirty miles an hour, there was a sudden lurch which threw us out of our seats and with a grinding of brakes the engine stopped, just two yards away from a dead end.   We discovered that some Malays had thrown over the switch and spiked it down in the hopes of wrecking the train in an old siding.

Every day I used to go out on inspection in a small four-wheeled trolley which was pushed along at about eight miles an hour by two Indian coolies, who ran behind with their bare feet, balancing themselves on top of the steel rail. The earthwork was done by Chinese coolies, working with a *changkol*, or kind of hoe, and two round baskets. The baskets were first filled with earth, then slung on the ends of a pole and carried up on to the bank. Practically all the brickwork was done by Sikhs, and the ironwork by Chinese. Our stone quarries were worked by Afghans, who are expert in the art of quarrying and breaking of stone.

These natives of Afghanistan were extremely interesting and struck me as being far superior to any of the other Asiatics that I met. Although they were living in the tropics they still retained the clothes of their native country and wore thick woollen garments, heavy boots, and thick stockings. Many of them had beards which they dyed a peculiar shade of red. They had a strange habit of wearing an ordinary man's shirt with baggy trousers and a waistcoat, but instead of tucking the shirt into the trousers, they left the shirt tails hanging out from under the waistcoat in a very ludicrous manner. Most of them were tall, well-built, and conscious of the fact that they were citizens of an independent kingdom, because their manner toward white men was entirely different from the cringing attitude adopted by the average Indian coolie. They were dignified, proud, haughty, and in some cases gave the impression that they considered themselves far superior to a white man. Being Mohammedans themselves, they got on splendidly with the Malays, who respected them. I must have had about two hundred of them altogether working for me. Their leader was named Samandar Khan.

Samandar Khan was a huge man, standing about six feet two inches, with a dyed beard. Whenever he came to see me upon business he carried a gold-headed walking stick and was accompanied by a servant. His manner of addressing me was at first annoying. I had become so accustomed to men bowing and scraping before me that I received a severe jolt when his servant appeared one day in my office and said: "My master wishes to speak to the 'assistant engineer'!" All the other contractors called me the *Tûan Besar*, that is, the Big Master; at least, they called me that in my hearing, but doubtless were less complimentary out of it.

I went out to meet Samander Khan who firmly but politely inquired how much longer I was going to keep him waiting before I went to his stone quarry and measured up his stone, and whether I had not yet received my instructions from my superior officer as to the necessity of keeping him regularly supplied with money for the payment of his labourers! In fact, he gave me a gentle calling down. Losing my temper I told him just what I thought of him, and when I had finished, he calmly gave me a little lecture on Afghanistan and reminded me that I wasn't talking to a miserable Indian, etc., etc. He did it in such a quiet and dignified way that I felt ashamed of myself for my outburst, and from that day onward I changed my methods.

On July 28, 1914, I received a cable from my wife to say that she had sailed from London and was on her way to join me. On August 5th, one of my telegraph operators rushed up to me and told me that England had declared war on Germany and that half the British fleet had been sunk off the mouth of the Thames! To say that I was stunned by the news but poorly describes my feelings, but as I look back now I can remember that I was filled with terrible anxiety, not only for my wife, but for England. Never before had I experienced that feeling of patriotism.

The news spread like wildfire, and as I walked down the village street of Tanah Merah, the only white man for miles around in the midst of a swarm of Asiatics, I felt a thrill of pride in the fact that I was an *orang puteh*.

Orang puteh means "white man," and it is strange that the British are the only "white men" in Malaya,

French are *orang* French, American are *orang* Americans, Dutch are often called *prut hijau*—that is, "green stomachs."

I had gone down to the village just to hear what the people were talking about, but instead of the subject of their conversation being War it was Milk. The canny Chinese tradesmen, within an hour of hearing that war was declared, raised the price of all food, and milk rose from eighteen to fifty cents a can. I immediately reported this to the British Adviser, and in a few days the Sultan of Kelantan issued a proclamation fixing the maximum prices of all foodstuffs. These proclamations were posted outside all the stores, and I myself placed one outside the Chinese store in Tanah Merah.

The Chinaman read it, promptly tore it down, and spat upon it. I asked for a can of milk at the government price; he refused to sell. I paid fifty cents and reported him to the police. The next day Captain Anderson, the Chief of the Police, and an Australian as distinguished from an Austrilian, appeared in Tanah Merah. He went at once to the Chinese shop, which by that time was surrounded by a mob of murmuring natives and other threatening Chinese. The shopkeeper was foolish enough to have decided already in his own mind that England had lost the war, and he adopted an insolent attitude, his nerve having been reinforced by the presence of an admiring crowd of his fellow shopkeepers. Grasping him by the scruff of the neck, Captain Anderson whisked him howling out of his store, forced his way through the crowd, and dragged him off to the railway station. There he bundled him into the train and took him to the capital of Kelantan, Kota Bharu, where he was tried, sentenced to be fined $500, and banished.

Only those who have seen what one white man can do in the face of a mob of hostile Orientals can realize what the power of British prestige used to mean in those days.

A few days after this occurrence I happened to meet the "Swiss" diamond merchant with the German name, in Kota Bharu. He was evidently pleased with himself and over-polite, I thought, and eager to know if I had any fresh news of the war. I asked him whether he had had any success with the Sultan, and he told me that he had sold him a diamond necklace for a fabulous sum of money, and added:

"What do you think I found them doing over there in his *estana*? They were lowering sacks full of silver dollars into a deep well!"

I asked whether the Sultan had mentioned the war, and he said:

"Oh, he is expecting Germany to win. Why, only this morning, when I was showing him my diamonds, the Sultan remarked: 'Explain to me once again, *tûan;* you tell me that England has a quarter of a million soldiers and Germany several million *orang German—tentu negri* Germany *misti menang!* [Germany is bound to win!]'"

The Sultan of Kelantan had been placed on the throne by the British Government after several of his predecessors had been mysteriously poisoned. He was surrounded by a crowd of hangers-on, little princes and big princes, murderers and brigands, many of them, and was said to be living in terror of his uncle who was supposed to have had a hand in the deaths of the other sultans.

The Sultan called me *Tûan Kretapi*—Master Railway—and was always very nice to me because he used to borrow my private inspection car whenever he wanted to take his wives out for a picnic by the sea at Tumpat.

One day I received an invitation to take breakfast with him. I sat on one side of him while his uncle, the suspected poisoner, sat on the other. The table groaned with all kinds of delicacies, including prehistoric eggs and durians. I noticed that the Sultan invariably offered his respected uncle each dish first before he helped himself, and if the uncle refused to partake, the Sultan did likewise.

That morning I saw the Crown Prince and heir to

the throne of Kelantan.   He was sitting at a separate table, surrounded by about half-a-dozen pretty and immaculately dressed boys about fourteen years old. The Prince himself, probably a little over twenty, was a thin, weedy-looking individual, almost white, with a sensitive face and long tapering fingers.   As he sat at the table he delicately toyed with a girl's embroidered handkerchief, which was highly perfumed, and behaved more like a girl than a boy, using a fan very gracefully and continually feeling to see if his hair was neat and tidy.   I understood that he was married to a pretty Malay girl, but that his affections were more set upon one of his boy attendants.   No matter where he went, whether to the theatre, or on a journey, or merely walking down the street, he was always accompanied by one or more of these boys.

This, of course, is an Oriental custom which Westerners do not appreciate.   The Prince's habits were not considered at all unusual by his own people. Many Malayan as well as Chinese boys are brought up as girls from babyhood, so that when dressed in girls' clothes it is impossible for a white man to detect the difference.   On the stage, especially among the Chinese, the so-called "actresses" are often men, and in the Malay Peninsula I myself have watched a *wayang* or play and been very much attracted by a pretty girl who turned out to be a boy!

Long before my wife arrived in Kelantan the German cruiser *Emden* was at the height of her activities and there was a grave doubt in my mind as to whether the steamer bringing her would ever arrive. It will be remembered that the *Emden* actually steamed into Penang Harbour in broad daylight and sank a Russian gunboat and a French torpedo boat before the eyes of the crowds on the water front. With his usual bravery and chivalry the captain of the *Emden* actually manœuvred his vessel into a position that ensured that no stray shells should fall into the city of Penang. After the Russian gunboat sank, the sea was dotted about with the floating bodies of Japanese girls.

Finally, after a voyage that lasted two weeks longer than usual and after being attacked by a submarine and chased by the *Emden*, the vessel bearing my wife arrived in Singapore. My joy can be imagined when one morning I went down to meet her at Tumpat and saw her waving to me from the bridge of the little white *Sapho*.

There were only two or three other white women in Kelantan at that time, and they were certainly very white when compared with the red cheeks that Luard (my wife) brought out from England.

We went straight to Tanah Merah where there was a royal reception awaiting her by the numerous contractors and officials.

CHAPTER XII

ONE of the most serious effects of the war was scarcity of money and material, so that it was only a few weeks before the work of construction practically ceased and I was transferred to a village nearer the sea called Pasir Mas, or Golden Sand, and placed in charge of the railway that was then in operation. My sojourn in Pasir Mas was one of the most exciting and interesting periods of my life.

In order to appreciate better the life we led, it will be necessary to give a few more details concerning the Malays themselves and the life they led. As I have said before, they have been called the gentlemen of the East, and they certainly have many gentlemanly characteristics. For instance, they are generally courteous and polite; usually they are more or less independent and hate any kind of work. In fact, the only real work that a Malay does of his own accord is to plough his ricefield.

The fields are divided into squares like a checkerboard by means of little mud walls called *battas*, about a foot high. When ploughing time comes, the heavy rain is prevented from draining away by means of these *battas* and the fields look like tanks full of water. The Malay catches one of his water buffaloes, or *kerbous*, attaches him to a wooden plough, which is often carved out of a single piece of wood and made by the same pattern that the Israelites used, and commences ploughing up the flooded fields. He ploughs and ploughs until the field is converted into a tank of thick mud about two feet deep.

While he is doing this, his wife has planted a little patch of dry ground with rice, placing the grains as closely together as possible, so that the rice grows up as thick as a tennis lawn. When this rice is about a foot high, she pulls it up in bunches, and after tying each bunch with a string, chops off the top. The women and children then wade out into the thick mud and plant the rice, one piece at a time, about four inches apart in fields that are often hundreds of acres in extent. When it is ready to reap, the women harvest it one piece at a time, cutting off the top of the rice with a knife and tying the tops up into little bundles.

All through the rice-growing season the fields swarm with snipe which migrate across the Peninsula at this time. Both the Malays and the Chinese say that the snipe never lay eggs and that they do not breed like other birds. According to the Malay the bird commences its existence as a tiny fish that is commonly known in ricefields and that has actually been known to come out of the sky with the rain (this is a fact). Eventually the fish turns into a bird in just the same way that a tadpole turns into a frog.

Snipe-shooting is one of the principal sports in Malaya, but it is often attended by a certain amount of risk on account of the fact that there are usually a few water buffaloes around, and these animals object strongly to the smell of a white man. I remember one smelling me when he was nearly half a mile away, but this is not as bad as the case of Mr. Stefansson, whom the polar bears smelled ten miles away.

One day I was tramping across a ricefield when I caught sight of a buffalo that had evidently noticed me. First of all his ears went back, then, holding his head with his nose stuck straight up in the air, he gave a funny complaining grunt and charged. I was rushing through the mud up to my knees, shrieking for help and with that huge animal just behind me, when suddenly a little naked Malay boy not more than six years old saw my danger, scampered out into the mud, seized the infuriated buffalo by the nose, and led it away from me.

Although the Malays are Mohammedans by religion, their Mohammedanism is by no means unadulterated by the paganism of the olden days. They are extremely superstitious people, and although many of them say their prayers five times a day like good Mohammedans, they do it only on three hundred and sixty-four days in the year, because once a year they propitiate the devil, presumably to keep on the safe side of him.

One day Sahar, who was not particularly religious, told me that there was going to be a ceremony of *Tola Bala*, or "propitiation of evil spirits," that evening, and offered to take me along with him. I wore my most brilliant sarong and at five o'clock in the evening started out across the ricefields. As I looked around me I could see little parties of Malays, men, women, and children, wending their way along the slippery *battas*. Soon we reached an open space on the bank of the Kelantan River, close to a native landing place, where there must have been more than a hundred Malays squatting on the grass, while others were arriving from all directions.

Each person was carrying a roast chicken fixed in a cleft stick in one hand, and a bowl of blood, entrails, and feathers in the other hand. Besides this, every person carried a small stick about two feet long, to the end of which was tied a little streamer of white cloth. Upon reaching the spot on the river bank, the roast chickens were piled up in a heap on one side, while the entrails, blood, and feathers were carefully placed in another heap on the very edge of the river bank.

As each person deposited his offering of blood and entrails, at the same time he stuck into the ground his little white flag.

By 6 o'clock there must have been about two hundred people present, squatting around the open space in which were piled the roast chickens on one side and the entrails surrounded by the little flags on the other. The evening breeze caused the hundreds of little flags to flutter like so many butterflies. When everyone was settled, the village *bomor*, or witch doctor, approached the heap of entrails with several lighted tapers which he stuck into the ground, all the time singing some weird chant in Malay. As soon as the chant was finished the sacrifice was offered up, which consisted in the crowd devouring the roast chicken and leaving the blood and entrails for the devil; not a bad idea!

By 6:30, every scrap of the roast chicken having disappeared, the people pulled up their little white flags and hurried home, never once looking back. Upon arrival at their houses, each Malay placed his little white flags, one for each member of the family, in a conspicuous position outside the house, as a sign to all evil spirits that the owner of the house had attended the ceremony of *Tola Bala*.

During the night, dogs and other animals devoured the blood and entrails, so that when morning came there was not a sign of the devil's share, which proved that the sacrifice had been accepted. The *bomor*, of course, receives an annual fee for this service!

I have attended quite a number of ceremonies at which devils were cast out of sick people who were thus apparently cured of illness by the witch doctor. Strangely enough, although the Malays know perfectly well that our doctors and medicine cure most of their illness, they go to a white doctor only as a last resort, and this leads to unfortunate results in many cases. It often happens that when they have practised all kinds of rites and administered many strange medicines to a sick person without succeeding in casting out the devil, they carry the dying person to a hospital or a doctor and ask for *obat* (medicine). If the hospital receives the patient and he dies, the *bomor* at once blames the white man's medicine and the wretched Malays think that perhaps after all they ought to have paid more money to their own *bomor* and not trusted to the hospital.

Among my own coolies I had all kinds of illnesses to attend to. When on survey work, and consequently out of reach of the *bomor*, the coolies regularly asked for my medicine, but once they were near one of their own villages, they preferred the devil-casting rites of the witch doctor.

I remember once hearing that one of my men was

dying, so I hurried to the coolie lines and found a young fellow rolling about in great agony and apparently delirious. Beside his bed was the *bomor* engaged in making a little model of the house in which the man was lying. The house was about a foot square and was fixed on to a nicely made little bamboo raft. I watched the old witch doctor as he carefully placed inside the house a cigarette, a complete outfit for chewing betel nut, a bowl of sugar, and a cup of tea. At 6:30, just as it was dark, he showed the house to the sick man and carried it down to the landing place on the river bank; then with a long pole he pushed the raft out into the stream and watched it float away. Having done this, he stuck into the river bank about a dozen little white flags, returned to the sick man, and reported what he had done. To my astonishment the sick coolie said he thought he felt better and the next day he was well!

The explanation of the cure is that evil spirits are supposed to live in the sea during the daytime, but at night they travel on the surface of the rivers, upstream, and land at the various landing places used by the Malays, causing sickness and bad luck in the locality. A good witch doctor is able to deceive the evil spirit by means of the model house, because, as it floats downstream, it eventually meets the spirit travelling upstream. The spirit recognizes the house, and upon entering it and finding plenty of good things to eat, remains inside and is carried by the river back to the sea. This is explained to the sick person, who very frequently is cured of his illness.

Once I saw an old woman who was obviously blind in both eyes being treated by the *bomor*. In this case the floating house had been ineffective, so another method was adopted. When late at night I slipped into an old house from which I had heard strange noises proceeding, I found the room packed with people of all ages, from tiny babies to old men. In the centre of the room was a large mat and squatting on it was the old blind woman. She was naked to the waist and beside her stood the *bomor*. At one side of the room was a large tray upon which there was a charcoal fire burning and various receptacles containing a variety of substances such as rice, lime, tobacco, betel leaves, and areca nut. There was also a Malay orchestra which played softly or furiously as commanded by the *bomor*. Every now and then he would cover her with a large bunch of leaves and then suddenly withdraw them. Again he would shout at her, scream at her, hit her, pinch her, and then fall on the ground himself in convulsions. For an hour, at least, this continued, while all the time the poor soul stared with her sightless eyes straight into space, making no sound or movement of any kind.

I was just about to slip out and go to bed when I heard the spectators crying: "*Tengok! dia lari* [Look! it's running away],"—referring presumably to the evil spirit. When I looked back I noticed the old woman's face twitching, then her shoulders, then her arms, and finally she began violently struggling on the mat until the *bomor* sprang to his feet and with one leap dived through the doorway of the house and ran screaming into the darkness. Everyone then began asking the old woman if she could see all right, but with tears rolling down her face, she replied: "Alas! this devil is too strong! I shall never see my children again." And inwardly I wished I were an eye specialist so that I could have operated on her for cataract, which I think was the cause of her blindness.

The Chinese have some very queer ideas of homœopathic remedies for various illnesses. I remember one night being kept awake by dreadful groans and the wailing of women until finally, getting out of bed, I walked outside and noticed a light burning in a little Chinese house not far away. I went over to the building and peeped through the cracks in the wall and saw a Chinaman lying on a bed groaning. He was on his back surrounded by five or six women,

Work is about the last thing a Malay wants. Rice cultivation is about the only labour he undertakes of his own accord except praying and minding the baby.

all of whom were vigorously massaging his stomach with tortoise-shell hair combs, which they heated in the smoky flame of a candle. When I pushed open the door and entered the room, no notice was taken of me, but the women kept on weeping and massaging. I asked what was the matter and the man's wife replied: "He ate some jungle beans for dinner to-night, and he has been getting fatter and fatter ever since!"

I noticed that the patient's stomach was distended enormously. I gave it a flick with my finger and it resounded like a drum, but I determined to make no offer of medicine until I was asked.

Adjoining the bedroom was the family shrine or *tokong*, which consisted of a red-and-gold picture of a venerable old man with long whiskers before which were several bowls of earth in which were stuck numerous joss sticks. The air was dense with the smoke of the smouldering incense and the shrine was thick with filth and the ashes of joss sticks which had burned there unceasingly for at least a generation. As a last resource one of the women suddenly thought of the shrine, but instead of praying for the man's recovery as I thought she was going to do, she began to sweep up the dirt and ashes from the floor. These she placed in a bowl of water and after a good stirring, administered it to her wretched husband. He gulped down the vile concoction and became fatter than ever! Then, having exhausted every cure they knew of, the women began imploring me to save the man's life.

I had already diagnosed the case as one of acute indigestion. I fetched the familiar paper packages containing Seidlitz powder and with due ceremony prepared to cast out the devil of indigestion. Experience had taught me that most natives will not drink medicine that bubbles. I decided the best thing to do would be to administer the Seidlitz powder in two parts separately dissolved in water. Nothing happened when my patient drank the first part, and the spectators looked very disappointed, but as I said the words "*Nanti dahulu, 'sat dia baik* [Wait a bit, he'll soon be well]," I administered the second part, and the effect was instantaneous.

Opening his mouth wide the Chinaman gave a very prolonged Ooooo!!!!! all the time becoming visibly thinner and thinner until, turning on his side and looking at me with a sickly smile, my patient said: "*Tûan tentu pandai!* [the master is certainly clever!]" Inwardly I thanked Heaven that he hadn't burst.

One of the most extraordinary customs prevailing among the Malays is the slow roasting of an expectant mother. The woman is placed upon a bamboo platform and a fire ignited beneath her, upon which earth is cast in order to make smoke. Here she lies in smoke and almost unbearable heat until the baby is born. The smoke is supposed to keep away evil spirits, and frequently the newly born infant is held in the smoke for the same purpose.

If a baby is troublesome, the mother places it on a square-shaped piece of black cloth and, using it as a cradle, hangs the baby underneath the house. Should the child continue to cry, the mother does not nurse it immediately but first takes a large stone called the baby's *ganti*, or substitute, and places it in the cradle before she lifts out the baby, so that in the event of there being an evil spirit near the cradle, it will be deceived by the *ganti* and think the child is still there, and consequently will not interfere with the little one while it is being nursed.

When a person dies, the door is left open to enable the soul to escape, and the soul is said to look exactly like the dead person but only about the size of the little finger.

One of my best friends among the Malays was an old man called Hadji Ismail. The title Hadji simply means that a man has made the pilgrimage to Mecca. Like most Hadjis, Ismail was a rascal, but at the same time a very interesting one. When I knew him, his son was about to make the pilgrimage himself and was taking with him the five longest strands of his sister's hair, who had just been betrothed.   Little pieces of gold were attached to the hair in order that it should sink when thrown down "Hagar's Well" in Mecca.   This celebrated well is said to contain holy water, and the Malays sometimes purchase a bottleful and bring it all the way home from Arabia to Malay in order that their relations shall have a drink and go to heaven.   It is said that after a drink the drinker often gets cholera and probably goes.

Cholera was rampant in Kelantan when Luard and I took up our abode in Pasir Mas, and night after night, as we sat on our veranda in the cool of the evening, we would hear the distant shouts of "*La illa ha ulla Allah* [There is no God but God]."   The words were spoken slowly at first by a large crowd of people, in perfect unison.   Gradually they spoke faster, louder and louder, the sound gradually dying away, only to be commenced again in a different direction.

From that weird noise, we could count the number of deaths and point them out to each other, saying: "There goes another over there!" and Luard would point west; then: "There goes another over there!" and I would point east.

Not only was cholera raging but the whole district was in turmoil.   There was no money to pay the contractors and consequently their coolies became alarmed and angry. Very soon all kinds of wild rumours began. England was defeated! The Germans were coming! No one would be paid for his work! The Government was bankrupt, and that explained the sudden issuing of paper money, even paper ten-cent notes!

There was no doubt that German agents had come into the country from Siam and were spreading all kinds of wild rumours amongst the natives. I was not at all surprised when Sahar came to me one day and said that his mother was sick, which was his way of expressing his desire to return to his home in Pahang. He secured for me a substitute called Omar, who was a local Malay, and thus Sahar passed out of my life. Besides Omar I engaged an assistant Chinese servant for Salleh, as we were now living in quite a large government bungalow and required a *tukan ayer*, or water-carrier. The *tukan ayer's* name was See Loo, and he turned out to be an extraordinary character. Every afternoon he would retire for several hours and I suspected him of smoking opium, until one afternoon, when I thought he was in dreamland, I went out to his sleeping quarters and to my astonishment I found him squatting on the floor with an Indian cobra in front of him. The snake was facing the man, and its hood was expanded, showing the spectacled markings of the common cobra, one of the deadliest reptiles in the world. Every now and then when See Loo slapped the snake's head, it would make a savage strike at him, only to be slapped again while the Chinaman jeered at it. He took no notice of me whatever but continued his game with the snake until suddenly he grabbed it and thrust it into a bag. By this time I was convinced that its fangs must have been removed, but when I said so, See Loo laughingly handed the bag to me and said: "See for yourself, sir." Not desiring to add another death to the twenty thousand that occur annually in India from snake-bite, I declined his kind offer, but mentally decided to test See Loo's ability as a snake-charmer at the first opportunity.

Only a few days afterward Luard and I were lying on our long chairs upon the veranda when I saw a snake about five feet long glide out of our dining room, cross the veranda, and descend the front steps. Whenever Luard saw a snake she became intensely excited and filled with desire to kill it. I never saw her show any fear of them, and this time she sprang up long before I did and followed the snake down the steps. Our house was built on concrete pillars, so that it was easy to walk about under the house. At the back, however, instead of being supported on a row of pillars, it was built on a solid brick wall to prevent any one in the front of the house

from seeing right underneath it and out to the servants' quarters at the back.   Completely surrounding
the house was a large brick drain.

The snake didn't like the look of the drain, and
instead of escaping, it turned and took refuge under
the house.   When I joined Luard there, I found that
she had driven the snake up against the wall where it
had turned and was coiled in its fighting position
facing her.   My thoughts instantly turned to See
Loo, especially when I recognized the snake as a
poisonous one.   Rushing behind the house I shrieked:
"See Loo, *ada ular besar, mari tankap sama dia* [See
Loo, there is a big snake, come and catch it]."

Out dashed the *tukan ayer*.   Without the slightest
hesitation he closed with the snake, and for an instant there was nothing to be seen but a mixture of
snake and See Loo's arms and legs.   Then I heard
the Chinaman's usual explanation of satisfaction:
"*Wah!*" and he held out the snake at arm's length,
squeezing its head until it opened its mouth and
showed its two almost transparent fangs.   With
great delight he popped the new snake into the same
bag as the cobra, and I frequently saw those two
snakes perform, apparently helpless in their efforts
to bite their captor.

Now that the war had put an end to the construction of the railway I was living in ease at Pasir Mas

as the district engineer in charge of the railway that was in operation, and at the same time I commenced the survey of a new line from Pasir Mas to Siam, which was only about twelve miles away, the border being the Golo River. The whole country was in a greatly disturbed state on account of war, cholera, and shortness of silver money, when a series of events occurred that added more fuel to the fire of unrest. Many of the rubber estates closed down and discharged large numbers of Chinese coolies, who began to overrun the district, form into bands, and commit gang robberies. Turkey had declared war, and there was a lot of talk as to what the Malays might do in the event of a Holy War. The next event, which was fortunate for England but a blunder on the part of Turkey, was the bombardment of Mecca, which resulted in the partition of Islam and the alliance between England and the King of the Hedjaz. I shall never forget the day I received the news that Mecca had been bombarded and that the High Shereef had denounced the Sultan of Turkey and proclaimed himself an independent monarch. The Malays would not believe a word of it and all through the war the average Malay remained faithful to the Sultan of Turkey and scoffed at the action of the High Shereef.

I have no doubt that in other parts of the Malay

Peninsula, where the sultans and rajahs were less independent and more Westernized, they knew the real facts of the case, but in Kelantan and Trengganu things were very different. Both these countries and their sultans were and still are about a century behind the rest of the country. The Sultan of Kelantan's chauffeur was an Austrian, his head boatman and captain of his motor yacht was a Turk called Osman, and there were many enemy aliens in the country. The attitude of the Malays showed a very marked change as time went on without much improvement in the financial situation.

For instance, whereas formerly it had been always customary for the crowds in the streets of Kota Bharu, the capital, to make way for any white man riding in a rickshaw, now they seemed intentionally to obstruct the roadway, and many were the growls and scowls as a European passed. I was in a position to notice the unrest more than were the other government officials, because I mixed with the Malays, and instead of parading in spotless white duck uniform, I frequently wore Malay costume myself. Every night we would have half-a-dozen or more visitors, sometimes Malay women to meet Luard or men to talk with me. Besides this, we were living many miles away from any town and were in the midst of a populous part of Kelantan.

One evening an old Chinese woman whom I had befriended, called Ah Mui, came to my house and warned us not to go out at night because she had heard that we might be attacked. I therefore engaged a Sikh sentry who stayed on guard from 6 o'clock at night until 6 in the morning. His name was Nigal Singh, and he drank a bottle of gin a day.

The next occurrence was one of those mysterious things that happen in the Orient. One evening, my new Malay servant, Omar, came to me and said: "*Semoar orang puteh sudah mati dalam Singapora*," which comforting news meant: "All the white people in Singapore are dead." In fact, the Malays in Pasir Mas were said to be discussing the Singapore mutiny before the news was known to the Kelantan government, and it was two days later when we heard officially that the Indian Regiment in Singapore had mutinied and murdered its officers and about thirty other people, including women and children. Instead of publishing the full facts, the censor allowed just enough news to leak out to cause the wildest rumours as to what really had occurred. I went about my work as usual, except that I carried a revolver upon instructions from the Chief of the Police.

The following little piece of hitherto unpublished history is interesting as illustrating the state of mind of the Malays and in particular of the Sultan of

Trengganu. The town of Kota Bharu is situated on the south bank of the Kelantan River and is connected with the railway, which is on the opposite side of the river, by means of a steam ferry. One day I received instructions to make a survey of the Kelantan River crossing and take soundings in the river right across the stream from Kota Bharu to the railway station on the opposite bank. In order to do this I anchored a series of boats at intervals across the river and stretched a long steel band from boat to boat. Whenever a vessel wanted to pass, it took only about three minutes for the steel band to be rolled up and thus remove any obstruction to navigation.

It happened one morning that I was taking an observation in the middle of the river when my boatmen cried out: "*Rajah Besar mari!* [The Big Rajah is coming!]" and when I looked up I saw coming toward us up the river a steam launch over which was flying the royal standard of the Sultan of Trengganu. Hussein was quite near the launch in a small boat holding a red flag and I heard him shout to the launch to wait until I had removed the steel band, but no notice was taken. I myself then stood up and shouted frantically to them to wait, but with a typical Malay yell from within, the launch, after crashing through the steel band, destroying it and upsetting one of the boats, continued gaily on its way.

I saw the Sultan of Trengganu sitting in his chair smiling, and with pardonable irritation I made a few remarks about his ancestry, à la American, and then shouted the same thing in Malay. I often wonder that the launch did not return and what it was that saved my life, because the launch did turn half round and my Malay coolies were terrified, but just as if someone on board had changed his mind, the vessel straightened out its course and left me cursing, surrounded by the wreckage of my surveying apparatus and the upset boat.

Many were the discussions and the guesses as to what transpired at the meeting between those two neighbouring sultans. Neither of them ever loved the British Government very much and this unusual meeting when the country was so unsettled gave rise to many rumours of rebellion.

During the daytime, in the country round about our bungalow at Pasir Mas, the Malays went about their tasks just as usual, but at night they met in bands to listen to some agitator, or to tear up the railway, or have a feast on stolen cattle! the simplest way of destroying the evidence of the theft. Every night there were the strange noises of distant gatherings, quite unlike the harmless drumming at a *ronging*, or native dance. There seemed to be a tense feeling in the air, and as Luard and I sat alone, miles away from any other white people, there was always a certain amount of satisfaction in hearing the steps of the sentry as he passed beneath our window.

We had gone to bed one night and had dropped off to sleep when we were startled by a furious banging on the door. Springing out of bed, dressed as I usually was, in a Malay sarong and *baju*, I went to the door. There, standing in the moonlight, was my telegraph operator who thrust into my hand a telegram, turned about, and ran away.

My feelings can be imagined when I read:

April 30, 1915
From the British Adviser, Kelantan
To the District Engineer, Pasir Mas
Adviser directs inform you native disturbance occurred Pasir Puteh. Extent not known. Recommend precaution you consider best.

While I was wondering what was best I heard a locomotive steaming past. I had previously received orders to keep up steam in the locomotives day and night in case of emergency, but I wondered where it was going without orders at that time of night. I went down to the railway station, which was close to my house, and there I saw the funniest sight imaginable.

Surrounded by all his household utensils, including his wife and numerous family, was the terrified station master. He was a Jafna Tamil and a Christian.

The telegraph operator had shown my telegram to everyone he met, with the result that the whole staff of the railway, with their wives and families, decided that Pasir Mas was getting a bit too exciting, and they were actually going to commandeer a special train and depart in peace for Tumpat, leaving me behind.

A few complimentary remarks restored the officials to reason, and we thereupon retired to the little Malay police station and held a council of war. The native police evidently knew far more about what had happened than I did, but they were careful not to say anything about Pasir Puteh. After some discussion we decided that if anything unusual happened in Pasir Mas, the engine drivers were to blow the whistles on the engines, which was to be the signal for the railroad officials to proceed to my bungalow where the police were to join us. What we were going to do them, I hadn't the faintest idea!

The next day I took my trolley and went to Tanah Merah to warn them there about the trouble at Pasir Puteh. When I returned to my house at Pasir Mas the place was silent. Luard had completely disappeared, also Omar and the two Chinese servants. Just when I was imagining all kinds of frightful things, one of the Malay policemen informed me that a motor boat had arrived from Kota Bharu and

I held a string in my left hand and thus photographed
myself after a touch of fever.

taken Luard away in spite of her vigorous protests. I took the train to the capital and learned that the Adviser had thoughtfully sent the motor boat for Luard and that she, together with all the other women and children, were then on their way to Siam. In fact, the crowded boat actually proceeded out to sea and after an exciting voyage dumped its human cargo on the sandy shores of Siam where they were taken charge of and sheltered until Kelantan quieted down.

Kota Bharu was in a state of the wildest excitement, especially when the Inspector of the Police marched out at the head of an "army" to meet the rebels who were then reported to be marching on the capital. The numerous Kelantan *tungkus*, or princes, were very much in evidence, swaggering through the streets in their best clothes, but it was reported that the Sultan had shut himself up in his palace and was slightly nervous because he heard that the leader of the rebellion was a distant relative of his named Tok Jangut. The name means "an old man with a beard," and he had a long beard right down to his knees—but it had only four hairs in it!

The first news from our "army" was that the police inspector who was in command had met greatly superior forces and had been forced to entrench. We then heard that Tok Jangut had proclaimed himself *kramat*—that is, especially protected by God and invulnerable. To prove it, the old man frequently came out in front of the trenches and allowed the "army" to blaze away at him without effect.

This news, which was found to be perfectly true, caused consternation in the Sultan's household, and it was reported that he asked the Adviser to send for assistance. Accordingly, the Adviser asked Singapore for help and it was announced in Kota Bharu that a man-of-war was on the way to Kelantan. Immediately, as the news spread, the Malays calmed down and waited expectantly for a steamer to arrive. Finding the disturbance was subsiding, someone is said to have reported "All's well" to Singapore with the result that the man-of-war was ordered to return! Unfortunately, the Malays were waiting with great interest for the ship to come. And when it didn't arrive they must have said, "There ain't no ship," because the disturbances broke out more violently than before. Here and there a bungalow was burned down, a coconut or rubber estate destroyed, a police station sacked and burned, and finally the people turned their attention to me in Pasir Mas.

One night, as I was lying awake, thinking of Siam, I heard a scuffle outside my bedroom window followed by a muffled splash, then dead silence. Snatching up my revolver I crept out but could see nothing. My heart was beating like a sledge-hammer and my knees were trembling when I heard a queer noise coming out of our well. We had a brick well six feet in diameter and fifteen feet deep in the garden. I walked over to it and peered down. I could not see a thing, of course, but I heard a hollow voice say: "Let down the bucket."

In amazement I lowered the bucket and when I hauled it up again, there on the end, still holding his rifle, was my sentry Nigal Singh!

He informed me that a party of Malays had thrown him down the well as a gentle hint that his presence was objectionable.

Singapore was now asked for help again, but they probably cried "Wolf," because it was more than a week before help eventually came. I happened to be staying at the Rest House at Tumpat, which is the seaport of Kelantan, when one morning I saw two vessels approach and anchor outside the surf. One was an old gunboat called the *Cadmus;* the other was a transport, I suppose. As I stood on a little wooden jetty I saw a boat put off and row toward the shore. It contained several British Army officers, all of whom had red tabs on the lapel of their coats, denoting that they were staff officers, I believe. One was a fiery individual with a very red face whom I took to be a general. I was dressed in my working clothes and was intensely interested in the martial display, when the "General" approached and said—well, I won't say what he said, but the gist of it was: "Who are you, sir?"

"The railroad engineer," I replied nervously.

"Well, haven't you got a revolution up here?" puffed the "General." "What the devil did you want me to do with the army?" indicating the ship out at anchor. "And where's the Adviser?"

I explained that the Adviser was probably in Kota Bharu, the capital, and that no doubt he would have been present to welcome the army if he had received a letter to tell him that one was coming. I saved the situation, however, when I explained that I would be very pleased to transport the army by train to the Adviser. Disembarkation commenced immediately.

First of all came huge piles of equipment, followed by two machine guns and several hundred soldiers, including a few men of the Royal Garrison Artillery and part of the Shropshire Regiment.

The R. G. A. men were old soldiers and as smart as ninepins, but the Shropshires—well, I never saw a weedier-looking lot of men in my life; but they had the latest rifles and were well equipped. After transporting the army to Kota Bharu, the "General" turned to me and said: "Take me to the Adviser."

Hot and angry he followed as I led the way to the British Residency, in front of which was a fine white flagstaff from which usually flew the Union Jack, but to-day there was no sign of a flag. Slightly irritated, the "General" said—well, I won't say what he said, but the gist of it was: "Where's the flag?"

I explained that the absence of any flag probably meant that the Adviser was "not at home." We returned to the town where we discovered that gentleman in conference with the manager of the Duff Development Company, who was a very important person in the eyes of the Sultan, because his company had concessions for practically all that was worth having in Kelantan. Meanwhile the army had encamped in Kota Bharu and all the bakers in town were baking bread for it. The "General," of course, was itching to face the foe, but the question of transporting the army's equipment and tents caused much delay on account of the fact that the only means of transport were bullock carts, and Malay bullocks, which are used to night work only, with remarkable sagacity refuse to work during the heat of the day even for a "general."

The soldiers were dressed in khaki uniforms, with

short trousers, puttees, and bare legs. It was suggested that they wear long trousers, as they had about thirty miles' march ahead of them, through jungle part of the way. But the idea of leeches troubling an army was pooh-poohed, and without waiting for the slow bullocks or changing their short trousers, the army set forth to battle. Before they had covered a dozen miles, practically the whole army was dispersed by leeches and sunburn, and while the men were removing the leeches and changing their trousers, the bullock carts passed by!

When the army had gone, I returned to my bungalow at Pasir Mas in company with a sergeant and five men of the Royal Garrison Artillery who were instructed to stay with me and "pacify the country." Upon arrival at home, I found several naval officers who were busily engaged with a chart and map of the sea coast. They had come to me to hear my version of the disturbances and to inquire as to the exact location of Pasir Puteh upon the map. It was soon apparent that the village was out of range but they thought that by causing their man-of-war to heel over slightly her guns could be elevated sufficiently to drop a few shells in the middle of the disturbed area around Pasir Puteh.

Thereupon they returned to H. M. S. *Cadmus* and by means best known to themselves succeeded in firing a few shells which dropped exactly on the desired spot. The terror and dismay of the rebels can be imagined when the heavens suddenly dropped such thunderbolts on them. The result was that the people fled from the entire district and when the army finally arrived there wasn't any enemy to fight!

Meanwhile the inhabitants of Kota Bharu were in a state of great anxiety, especially the Sultan. With the departure of the army he had locked himself up more securely than ever and was probably expecting every minute to hear of the arrival of Tok Jangut at the head of a victorious Malay army.

Under these circumstances, the Sultan is said to have demanded that he be given some British soldiers to guard him, and about half-a-dozen "Tommies" were detailed to act as sentries outside his palace.

One day, his Majesty cautiously peeped through the cracks in the wall of his domain to inspect his British bodyguard and was much disgusted to observe what very insignificant little knives the sentries carried on the ends of their rifles. Being unused to such a weapon as a bayonet, the Sultan decided to summon to his assistance and protection his own royal bodyguard. Accordingly, messengers went forth secretly into the night, east and west and south and north, to summon his array, and a few days afterward, while the six sentries were wondering why on earth their presence was necessary, they beheld advancing toward them what appeared to be a motley mob of Malays, armed with spears, krises, long swords, and old rifles. It was the Sultan of Kelantan's bodyguard hastening to his protection!

Unfortunately the Tommies said to themselves, "This must be old Tok Jangut himself and his army at last." With fixed bayonets and a British yell they charged the enemy and dispersed the Sultan's bodyguard, returning from their very successful encounter with arms full of spears and krises, many of which are now in my possession.

But let us see what was happening in Pasir Mas. By a strange coincidence, the sergeant and the five men of the Royal Garrison Artillery who were stationed at my house turned out to be regular London cockneys. Two of them actually came from Barnes, the town where I was born. They told me that my father, who was the churchwarden, had frequently turned them out of church for misbehaving. This made a real bond between us and they called me a "Townie," meaning that I came from the same town.

My cellar was full of beer and other beverages, besides cases of canned food from Singapore. The soldiers' food allowance consisted of one can of corned beef and three large biscuits a day, and so, when I showed them my cellar and gave them free use of it,

their joy was exceeded only by the size of their appe-
tites.

One evening the sergeant informed me that as his
orders were to "pacify the country" he had decided
to issue a proclamation forbidding any one to be
out-of-doors after sunset without carrying a light.
The fact that even if his proclamation had been
printed in the Malay language instead of in English
the majority of the people could not have read it
made no difference, and so the proclamation was
posted with due ceremony.   The sun set at about
6.30 and at 7 o'clock the sergeant and his four men
commandeered a locomotive in which they rode up
and down the line, occasionally taking a pot shot at
someone without a light, usually aiming at the lower
regions.   Very often they returned home with several
chickens impaled upon their bayonets.

One night, while the men were joy-riding on one of
the engines and I was in bed, a crowd of Malays
surrounded my house and commenced throwing
lighted torches on the roof! Fortunately, being a
government roof, it was made of asbestos, and when
they found it was especially protected by God, the
men turned their attention to some of the coolie
houses in the station yard, which burned beautifully,
as did also the railroad brickyard buildings.

Night was turned into day, and in accordance with

our plan of action, all the available whistles in the station yard commenced blowing a continuous blast. Everyone rushed to my bungalow as arranged, excepting the Malay policemen, and when I went to the police station to investigate the cause of their delay, I found that the blowing of the whistles had been the signal for the policemen, after discarding their uniforms and rifles and leaving them thrown about the floor of the police station, to disappear into the wilds. In the midst of the turmoil the engine containing the five pacifiers arrived, and together we advanced on the burning brickyard, where the figures of numerous Malays could be seen, sharply silhouetted against the flaming buildings.

We had to cross over an iron bridge on the way. As we did so a volley from the Malays greeted us, and several bullets whizzed unpleasantly close to my head. The sergeant dragged me down, and as we lay on our faces his men returned the fire and the enemy retired, carrying with them several wounded or dead. When news of these disturbances reached the ears of the Singapore Government, the Hon. George Maxwell was sent to investigate. After visiting me at Pasir Mas, he decided to pay a visit to Pasir Puteh and find out personally whether Tok Jangut was really invulnerable or whether his survival for so long was merely due to rotten shooting.

Mr. Maxwell is a typical British sahib, whose name is familiar as the author of several delightful books upon Malaya. Shortly afterward I was told that he was walking across a ricefield on his way to Pasir Puteh when the Malays led by Tok Jangut opened fire, and that Maxwell himself shot Tok Jangut very successfully which, if correct, is not surprising, as Maxwell is one of the finest big-game shots in the world. This little engagement happened a few days after Luard had returned to Kelantan from Siam.

One morning while we were sitting at tiffin in the Rest House at Kota Bharu, an automobile stopped outside and the driver called out: "Come and see what I have on the back of my car!"

Luard ran out, and there, tied on the trunk carrier, was the ghastly body of Tok Jangut! As soon as the Sultan heard that the rebel was really dead, he ordered him to be exhibited on a gibbet, suspended by his feet, as an object lesson to others. Thus ended one of those numerous little disturbances that occurred in many parts of the British Empire during the war. As I write about it now, it seems like a chapter from "Alice in Wonderland," but when it happened it was very different.

CHAPTER XIII

SOON after the events recounted in the last chapter I received an offer of a two-year agreement to survey roads for the Government of Kedah, the native state adjoining Kelantan on the northwest. On account of the mountain ranges between these two states, it was necessary to make the long journey by sea, down the East Coast and then up the West Coast of the Peninsula to Penang, in order to reach Kedah. From Penang I took the train to Alor Star, the capital of Kedah, where I reported to the State Engineer.

Kedah is one of the most progressive of the Malay States, although it does not belong to the Federation. The country is not only rich in tin, but produces a great deal of rice, rubber, and tapioca. It is not long since Kedah was under Siamese control, and the native population is still largely Siamese. Many of the villages are queer mixtures of Siamese and Malays, and I came across one in which, although the people were Mohammedan Malays, they spoke only Siamese, and although they did not keep pigs as the

Siamese do, they frequently mingled with the Siamese monks in a neighbouring *wat*, or Buddhist monastery.

I soon discovered that the reason the services of a railroad engineer had been requisitioned by the Public Works Department was that they were having considerable difficulty in getting any good roads surveyed on account of the swampy and hilly nature of the country. Since I am one myself, I must be pardoned for thinking that a railroad engineer is usually a far better surveyor than the average Public Works engineer, who is supposed to be a "jack of all trades" and is rarely a master of any.

The State Engineer of Kedah was an architect by profession and knew as much about road surveying as I did about architecture, which was very little. The first job he gave me was to survey a road from Kedah's highest mountain, Gunong Gerai, to a village in the interior called Sik. As we sat in his office with a map of Kedah before us, I noticed at once that there were numerous blank spaces on the map which denoted that the country had not been surveyed, and I was very much amused at the bland way in which the architect showed me with his pencil how easy it was going to be to survey a road across such "open country." He quite casually said: "After you get to Sik, I would like you to go to a

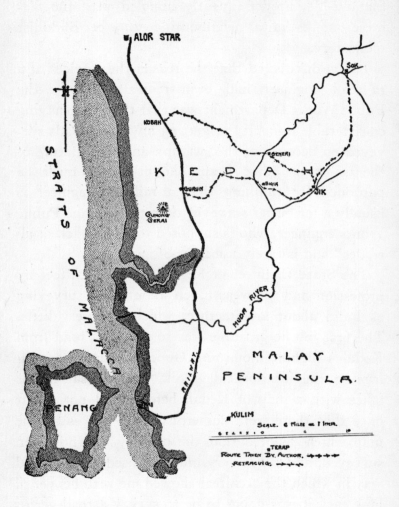

place I have heard of called Sok; they say that elephants go there to die!"

I think he imagined that I was another Harry Franck, and that it would be a mere detail to vagabond my way through country that was absolutely unexplored. However, the prospect of some real exploration appealed to me, and as I left the State Engineer's presence, I had considerably more confidence in my own ability than when I entered.

Gunong Gerai is the magnificent mountain that is so plainly visible from Penang where it is called Kedah Peak. At the base of the mountain is a village called Gurun, and it was from Gurun that I started my survey to Sik.

Just before my departure I met a man who was about to ascend the mountain in search of a particular kind of cockroach which is found only there; he told me that he expected to spend about six months doing nothing but hunt this unfortunate cockroach. As I had no desire to spoil his sport, I refrained from telling him that the mountain was infested with tigers of a particularly ferocious kind as well as cockroaches.

I met in the same village an American doctor who was hunting a particular kind of mosquito and had been doing so for years. He requested me to send him specimens of mosquitoes in empty match boxes, which I did, and thus found the only use I ever had for an empty match box. I asked him what was the best thing to do in order to prevent malarial fever on such a place as a rubber estate. He said there were two recognized ways of combating the disease: one was to clear away the vegetation from all ravines, and the other was not to disturb the vegetation in any way. Both methods are now largely used in the Malay Peninsula with equal success.

To accompany me on the journey I took Hussein and ten picked Malay coolies. We started across the ricefields, which were full of women and girls, reaping the rice one piece at a time with knives about an inch long and tying it into bundles. In the middle of one field, perched up on piles about ten feet from the ground, was a little house. Inside it, lying on his back, was a boy about ten years old and attached to his big toe was a string which passed out of the doorway. From the end of the string, radiating in all directions over the field, were about thirty more strings and on the end of each was an empty kerosene can perched on a high pole. Every now and then the boy gave a kick, which caused all the empty cans to rattle and frighten away the hundreds of rice birds that were busily stealing the crop.

The heat as I crossed that field was so great that the water in which the rice was growing was not merely warm, but unpleasantly hot. In the distance was the

Bamboo forests have taken the place of the original jungle in many places; they are a great obstacle to the surveyor.

jungle, bright green and of very irregular height, the average height of the trees being about one hundred and twenty feet with here and there towering above the rest a monster tree more than two hundred feet high. The trunks of these immense trees were the only ones visible and they looked as if they had been white-washed! Upon some of them there was a patch of scarlet or purple flowers which indicated the presence of some flowering vine. Here and there were trees that appeared to be completely covered with flowers, but on closer inspection these proved to be not flowers but new foliage which eventually would turn green. New leaves in the jungle are often pink, violet, or blue. From outside the jungle looked impenetrable, but this outside layer of vegetation was unusually dense on account of its exposure to the light.

No sooner had we started cutting into it than there was the cry *"Peningat!"* which means a certain kind of small wasp. I needed no interpreter, because in the next few minutes I counted no less than thirteen wasp stings on my right hand alone and found that I had knocked down a little wasp nest that had been suspended beneath a big leaf. Thirteen has always been my unlucky number. We tied a bunch of dead leaves to the end of a long stick, set it on fire, and burned the nest.

The jungle at this place was called "secondary"

growth and it was so dense that it was impossible to walk through. Every foot had to be cut and it took all the morning to go half a mile. Finally we struck an ancient elephant track about two feet deep. The earth had been worn away by the elephants' big toenails, the jungle had been neatly cleared to a height of about ten feet, and there was a regular tunnel through the trees. I discovered that it was a well-known elephant track that continued for many miles until it lost itself in the hills of Siam. Later I surveyed it and it is now marked on the most recent maps of the country.

My companions followed the elephant track, but sometimes I wandered off into the jungle, keeping myself in touch with them by shouting. The farther into the jungle we penetrated, the larger became the trees, but the undergrowth diminished, and after a while we were passing through virgin jungle. The dense undergrowth had given way to a very slight one through which it was fairly easy to walk by cutting down a bush or a vine here and there. The ground was covered with masses of beautiful iridescent fern that changed colour like silk and sometimes, high up among the tree trunks, gliding gracefully along with only an occasional flap of its wings, we caught sight of a huge butterfly. The ground was damp and springy, full of roots and decaying leaves; the atmosphere was like that of a hothouse and there was a smell of damp soil in the air. But compared with a temperature of anything up to 160 degrees outside in the sun, it felt cool here where the temperature was practically constant at eighty degrees.

One morning I came across a large dead trunk about two feet thick and about fifty feet high. In my innocence I tried to push it over, when something fell on my head, smashed my helmet over my eyes, and covered me with dust. About two feet of the tree-top had broken off. Fortunately for me it was no longer wood but a mass of earth and ants.

Another day the coolies stopped cutting and, refusing to continue, pointed to a bush and said: "*Baniak susa*," which means "much trouble." To encourage them in overcoming such trifling difficulties I myself started cutting down the bush. It went down easily, but suddenly I jumped! Something had bitten me! Then it seemed as if I were being bitten all over, and I started tearing at my hair and carrying out all kinds of acrobatic feats, much to the amusement of my coolies. The bush contained a nest of ants and I was simply covered with them, big red ones half an inch long. Pulling them off did not relieve me in the least, because although I could pull their bodies off their heads remained on and continued to bite me. That one experience taught me a lot of Malay and I have no doubt that the Malays picked up a lot of English.

One morning, to my surprise, we emerged into a large clearing in the jungle in the middle of which was a fine house with a white man standing on the steps. He was a pioneer rubber planter and welcomed another white man with joy. It was about luncheon time, I remember, and I was delighted when he yelled: "Boy, bring the master a whisky and soda and a gin and bitters for me; afterward bring luncheon."

He invited me to spend the night at his house, but explained that I would have to entertain myself because he was about to start down the river for supplies. Before leaving he entrusted to my care his large St. Bernard dog and a canary! Before going to bed I was most careful to lock the bird in the mosquito room and chain the dog to his kennel just outside the kitchen door. That night I slept in a bed for a change and slept soundly. The next morning I went downstairs to unchain the dog, but all that was left of him was his head in the collar and leading off into the jungle were tiger marks! I thought: "Good Heavens! What about the blessed canary?" and rushing into the house I entered the mosquito room. There was the cage but there was no canary! But on the floor, fat and contented, was my friend's cat, which I must have overlooked when I had so carefully placed the cage there on purpose to avoid the animal. I remembered those thirteen stings, and I left the house, cursing my luck. I have not seen my host since!

Before I left Alor Star, the State Engineer instructed me to carry about a rain gauge. I had almost despaired of finding a space in the jungle large enough to use it that was not more or less protected by the trees, when one day I came to an open space which looked very much like a portion of a ploughed field. It was a natural "salt lick." The ground was covered with the tracks of all kinds of animals who secured their supply of salt by licking the ground or by eating the soil. Here I placed the rain gauge at about midday and started back to camp. It rained from 12:30 to 3:30 that afternoon, and when I examined the gauge the next morning, it registered nine inches for the three hours! As a matter of fact, the rainfall in Malay varies from one hundred and fifty to two hundred and fifty inches annually, so that nine inches in three hours was just a shower.

Of all the numerous obstacles in the jungle, I consider the swamp to be the worst. Kedah is noted for its enormous swamps which, to quote Yorkshire, "would drown a bloody duck."

Most people's conception of a swamp is a place full of reeds and water, but there are no reeds or grass in most jungle swamps. As a general rule, a Malay swamp consists of dense jungle growing in deep slimy ooze which is often apparently bottomless. Growing in this fearful muck is a peculiar kind of palm tree called by the Malays *klubi*. The *klubi* palm is protected by fan-like clusters of poisonous thorns, usually about five thorns in one cluster. So sharp are these thorns that they pierce one's boots instantly, and since they are very brittle they break off, leaving their poisonous points deeply imbedded in one's flesh. The only way to cross such swamps is to build a wooden *titi*, or bridge, usually consisting of one or two tree logs passing from the roots of one large tree to those of another. We built miles of these *titis*. When a road is finally built across such a swamp, either a permanent bridge has to be constructed or else earth is thrown upon a mattress made of trees and eventually a road is made that is literally floating in the swamp. The problem before an engineer is, of course, to find the shortest possible crossing of such a swamp, and this entails making a survey of its boundary. On one occasion I surveyed more than eighteen miles around the edge of a swamp before I succeeded in finding a place to cross, and when the crossing place was found, it was less than a hundred feet in width! In fact, these peculiar swamps look like very complicated jigsaw puzzles when drawn upon a plan.

Sometimes long before reaching a swamp the noise of a million frogs could be heard, but the instant we entered the water it stopped and we would pass through a district that was swarming with frogs without seeing or hearing a sign of life. In such districts the trees were often smothered with moss and all kinds of other plants. Every now and then we would find a large palm with some kind of fruit upon it, but I noticed that the palms with the nicest fruit were always protected by murderous-looking thorns, many of which were more poisonous than *klubi*.

Beware of asking a Malay if a fruit is eatable, because he always says, "yes," and then perhaps he will add: "But it is very poisonous." The only safe way is to watch the monkeys, and if they eat the fruit it cannot be very poisonous. I tried this once when I came to a large tree full of monkeys eating fruit. I tasted some myself, found it perfectly vile, and concluded that the monkeys must have been eating it for medicine! Palm trees with trunks are not at all common in the jungle, and when they do occur they rarely grow more than fifty feet high. They were usually overshadowed by the main jungle trees.

About halfway between Gurun and Sik we had to cross the Muda River. Since there were no boats available, we made a raft. One morning, soon after, I heard a strange whistling noise high up in one of the trees and noticed a pretty little windmill, rotating rapidly and at the same time whistling. Soon we saw these musical little windmills on many other trees, and Hussein said to me: "*Ada orang Siam!* [There are Siamese!]"

Just as he spoke, one of the other Malays shouted: "*Gaja!* [Elephant!]" and there, coming toward us, was a huge elephant with magnificent tusks. There were three people on it: one was the driver, a Siamese, who sat astride the elephant's neck and guided him by kicking him occasionally behind the ear; behind him, seated underneath a sunshade, was a Buddhist monk dressed in a flowing yellow robe and accompanied by a little Siamese boy about ten years old. They took no notice whatever of us, but continued past us and disappeared into the gloom of the jungle. A few moments afterward I heard my coolies swearing and making very uncomplimentary remarks about Siamese people in general, and when I caught up to them they were held at bay by an old sow, with a litter of about sixteen little pigs. Siamese pigs are disgusting to look at, as their backs have usually collapsed because of the weight of their stomachs which they drag on the ground. They are never fed; consequently they are living garbage and sewage destructors. I fired my revolver and they dashed off into the jungle in terror.

Soon we came to a beautiful open space about fifty yards square, completely covered with sparkling white sand and surrounded with coconut and *pinang* trees. On one side of the square was a well-built wooden house, beautifully carved, a typical Siamese *wat*. Seated around the doorway were seven or eight monks with shaven heads, dressed in bright yellow and chewing betel nut. Around the monks, but at a lower level, were a number of Siamese women with dishes of food and other offerings which they brought daily to the *wat*. Each monk had a boy attendant who received the presents and disappeared with them inside the buildings.

One of the monks was evidently the head of the *wat* because he sat apart and was treated with great reverence by the others, especially the Siamese women. He was a fine-looking man about fifty years old, with a keen, intelligent face and charming smile, which divulged a scarlet mouth and teeth jet-black from incessant chewing of betel nut.

Hussein could speak Siamese fairly well, and so together we approached the chief monk, whose name was the Tok Sami Bigia. When Hussein began speaking Siamese to the Tok Sami, the latter smilingly replied in Malay. I explained that I was surveying a road to Sik and that I had come to ascertain the Sami's wishes as to where he would like the road to be! He was pleased and flattered and not only indicated where he would like the road, but gave me a Siamese guide to help me survey it. He also invited me to stay at the *wat* as long as I liked and gave me a special little house adjoining the main building. His only request was that I should give instructions to my Chinese cook that no chickens were to be killed anywhere near the *wat*.

For several days I was conscious of being carefully observed and I was most careful for my part to do nothing that might offend the old priest. Every afternoon I invariably had tea served in my house and I could see the monks watching me with great interest as I placed sugar and cream in it.

One afternoon I invited the Tok Sami to have tea with me, and he came, accompanied by his boy attendant. I handed the cup of tea to the boy who handed it to the Sami. He drank it with relish and before leaving explained that he was allowed to drink but not to eat anything during the daytime. Every day he came for his afternoon tea and we became so friendly that one day he confided to me: "There is a very nice Siamese girl in Bigia. If you will marry her, she can live in this house and then you can settle down here permanently!" I asked to see the girl first, and sure enough he sent for her—a young Siamese girl, almost white, about eighteen years old. She could not speak Malay, but when the Sami asked her if she would marry me she seemed quite willing. However, as I thought that to be properly married, even according to Buddhist rites, might lead to complications, I made my excuses and the old monk said: "I think you are wise; women are very troublesome, are they not?"

I was interested to learn that all the Siamese either had entered or would enter the monastery as novices. Most of them, of course, return to ordinary life, but a certain percentage become monks.

A few days after my arrival at the *wat* I heard that about sixty boys and girls were to be initiated and that a celebrated Buddhist priest was coming all the way from Bangkok to officiate. For nearly a week the monks were busy with huge rolls of white cloth which they first dyed yellow and then made into robes. One evening, six large elephants arrived, each carrying about three monks, and on the last elephant came the priest from Bangkok. He continually held a fan in front of his face. The next day I was invited to attend the ceremony in the *wat*, for which, many weeks beforehand, the novices had been carefully preparing, learning and practising their chants and responses, which sounded exactly like Gregorian music. Besides this they had made for themselves elaborate "begging bowls," symbolical of their absolute poverty. There were dozens of marvellously decorated candles of solid beeswax, besides all kinds of strange decorations beautifully made from coloured paper and tinsel.

At night, as I sat on the outskirt of the crowd of parents, watching the ceremony of initiation, I couldn't help thinking at once of a solemn, high mass. Seated beside a golden image of Buddha, which was not more than two inches high, was the chief priest, facing the congregation with a fan still held in front of his face. Standing before the Buddha were six of the older monks, and squatting behind them were the sixty novices. It was impossible to tell boys from girls because their heads were all shaved.

The incessant chanting and responses continued all night, and the next day the novices were carried, each one on the shoulders of a man, to a tall pagoda-like structure, where they were seated in rows, one above the other. Then the crowd of parents and friends rushed down to a stream and returned with buckets of water with which they baptized them. Baptism was practised, of course, long before the Christian Era. This ceremony continued until the novices were drenched to the skin and shivering with cold, and then they were carried back to the *wat* and disappeared inside.

Hussein told me one evening that the Tok Sami was a magician and could see through anything. When I asked the Sami whether he could see through anything, he replied that he could. I asked if I might test him; he smilingly consented, and I produced from my pocket the Chinese gambling dice game that I have already described called Main Po. Taking a pencil I drew out on the floor of the *wat* the square with two diagonals and placed the brass box containing the dice in the middle. I then gave it a good spin. "Where is the red?" I said to the Sami. Looking intently at the brass box he said: "There," and when I opened the box I was dumbfounded to find he was right. Thinking that it was a lucky guess, I tried again. But again he located the red. I tried him about a dozen times without his making a mistake, until he grew tired and refused to continue. When I asked him why he did not go down and break the bank at the gambling house, he said: "Ah! But I am not allowed to gamble."

I wrote to my wife who at this time was living in

Alor Star and told about the Tok Sami. Several months afterward, when I was far away in the interior, the old priest paid a visit to her at Alor Star. Remembering my story about Main Po, Luard asked him to show her how he could see through brass! And he performed the feat just as successfully as before.

After leaving the *wat* we continued for three weeks, cutting our way through the jungle until we arrived at Sik which was nothing more than a small Malay village. It will be remembered that I had been instructed to visit a place called Sok, which was supposed to be a dying place for elephants. When I made inquiries about it at Sik, I was told that the best place to get such information was at a village called Generi, which is shown upon the map on page 190. I had not intended to stay in Sik more than a few hours, but when I was about to leave several of my coolies complained that they were *sakit*, which means sick. I knew perfectly well that all they wanted was to be sick in Sik so that they could have a good time; I gave them each half a cup of castor oil and the day off.

The next morning there were no more invalids and we started on our journey to Generi. As the road survey had ended at Sik, I was able to make fairly rapid progress to Generi by following ancient elephant tracks most of the way. The jungle was apparently virgin, and in the dim light we could see great vines passing from tree to tree. Very few of these vines had leaves upon them, and some were hanging loosely from some branch a hundred feet above my head. Often at the first forked branch of a tree there was a huge fern with its graceful fronds hanging fifteen feet down or else a weird-shaped orchid plant.

Jungle trees are nearly always provided with enormous buttresses to support them in the rotten soil. In one case I actually measured the base of a tree and found that the buttresses were thirty feet across. Ten feet from the ground this same tree was only eight feet thick. The great exception to the rule is the *jelutong* or wild rubber tree. These trees are by no means common, and if we came across one the coolies would stop to amuse themselves by slashing the bark with a knife and watching the thick white *latex* run out and coagulate almost at once. The wood of the tree is soft and white and makes excellent drawing boards.

Our progress was sometimes stopped by a tree which the Malays called "Compass." The reason for the name is that the tree cannot be felled with an axe, and a compass has to be used to survey around such a tree. The wood is useless because it decays rapidly.

Sometimes we passed through a forest of bamboo, one of the most interesting and useful jungle products. It is an excellent illustration of the rapid growth of plants in a tropical climate. A bamboo shoot will grow about an inch an hour, and the Chinese and Malays have both been known to utilize this remarkable growth for torturing captives. They tie a man down on top of a young bamboo shoot which in a few hours begins slowly but inevitably to grow up into the victim's body.

It is hard to say what the natives would do if they were deprived of this plant. It is used for water vessels, cooking pots, and making fire by friction, for building houses and weaving mats, for fish traps, kites, hair combs, and many kinds of musical instruments, including the xylophone, the Jew's harp, and the flute. The jungle dwarf uses it for his blowpipe and for making all kinds of traps. The Chinese use it for water pipes, and I have seen a bamboo pipe line more than a mile long. In fact, the uses of bamboo would fill a large book.

Another very useful jungle product is *rotan*, or rattan. This is a creeping palm that grows to a prodigious length; specimens more than eight hundred feet long have been found. It is extremely strong and is used instead of rope by the Malays, especially for tying their houses together in con-

If you want a thrill, make a journey downstream on a bamboo raft, shooting the rapids. This is a common means of transport in the interior.

struction. *Rotan* is exported in large quantities to America and Europe where it is used for making baskets and for caning the seats of chairs.

Two days after leaving Sik we reached Generi, which consisted of a few scattered houses and scarcely deserved to be called a village. Here I was able to obtain some definite information about Sok. I was told that the headman of the village was spending a few days at a place called Dusun Durian, which means a group of durian trees. The trees were pointed out to me about half a mile away across the paddy fields, and even at that distance the durians could be seen distinctly, hanging like footballs on the branches.

As I approached the trees the terrific odour of the fruit became stronger and stronger. Then I came to a small space in the jungle which had been neatly cleared of all bushes and undergrowth and carefully fenced around in order to keep out animals. Just inside the fence was a small Malay house and in the middle of the space were three large durian trees about a hundred feet high. Outside the house was a pile of ripe durians, and they were the cause of the smell.

The owner of the house was an old man who was the village *penghulu* or headman. When I asked him if he knew of any place around there where elephants were supposed to die he smiled and said:

"Not where they die, but where they go when they *think* they are going to die! Sok is an elephant's *health* resort!"

It is curious that no one seems ever to have found the dead body of an elephant, at least one that has died from natural causes. This has given rise to a superstition, common among natives, that elephants have secret places to which they retire when they feel death approaching. Sok was evidently such a place, because the old *penghulu* told me that I would find hot water bubbling out of the ground and that the water contained *obat* or medicine.

I tried to hire some elephants from him but he said that only large tuskers could make the journey to Sok safely, because wild elephants often came out of the jungle and attacked the small tame ones. This sounded exciting, but as all the local elephants were without tusks, I had to make the journey on foot without meeting anything more dangerous than leeches. The ground near the springs was literally covered with elephant tracks, but not a sign of a dead one. After taking a sample of the water for analysis I returned to Generi and decided to hire the elephants there and cut across country to the nearest station on the railway, which was about twenty miles away. I bargained with the owner to pay him when we arrived at the station, and for the next seven hours I slid around on the elephant's ribs until at last I heard the shrill whistle of an engine. The elephants heard the whistle, too, and before I knew exactly what had happened, I was sitting in the mud with my baggage all around me! I never knew that an elephant could buck like a broncho! But those two elephants with their owners dashed off into the jungle and I never saw them again.

Within a few hours I was sitting in the club in Alor Star, dressed in a white suit and enjoying a gin sling. The recipe for a gin sling is as follows: Take a wineglass full of the best gin and to it add the juice of a fresh lime. Add one teaspoonful of cherry brandy and sugar to taste. Shake up well with crushed ice and soda water and drink in a long glass.

CHAPTER XIV

AFTER I had been in the Malay Peninsula for four years without a change of climate, I began to get malarial fever so badly that the attacks would recur even when I was taking single doses containing thirty grains of quinine. I was given hypodermic injections of quinine, which is a painful treatment, and finally effervescent quinine, which in my opinion is by far the pleasantest way to take it, but nothing seemed to stop the fever from coming back again worse than ever.

One of the most interesting jobs I ever had in Kedah was the survey and construction of a main road from Parit Buntar to Kulim, passing through a place called Terap. When I first made the exploration survey I had to wade and often swim across swamps day after day. It was eventually decided that I should make a permanent camp at Terap and take charge of the construction of the most difficult part of the road I had surveyed. I was allowed to have a large bungalow constructed, but as there were no roads for many miles no building materials could be transported, and the bungalow had to be built en-

tirely of jungle produce from its hardwood foundations to its nipa roof.   Even the blinds were made of
bamboo strips.

Terap is situated in the midst of a very hilly district, and frequently in the morning and evening the
house was enveloped in clouds. Talk about rain!
Nine inches in three hours was ordinary and many a
day the rain gauge which was made to record ten
inches would overflow in considerably less than three
hours. The rain always brought out armies of insects and moths, and as soon as I lit a lamp, thousands
of flying ants invaded the house and in a few minutes
the glass chimney of the lamp choked up with ants
and the light was out. The ants had a nasty habit
of breaking off their wings and falling to the ground,
where one would take hold of another by the tail
until a line of about six or more were attached head to
tail. Then they would crawl all over the house like
little living strings of sausages! I had to buy a
special kind of lamp designed to keep the insects out.
The ants could not burn themselves on it but they
settled on the globe in thousands. There they
promptly broke off their wings, which fell on my dining table; I placed a large basin beneath the lamp and
within a couple of hours it was full to the brim with
wings!

I spent one evening after the rain in my mosquito

room. This room was four-sided and made entirely of fine copper gauze. One side of the room was attached to the side of the house, but I had purposely placed gauze on that side as well, because the Malay insects were so intelligent that when there were only three sides to the mosquito room they used to enter the house, go to my bedroom, crawl through the cracks in the wall and thus enter the mosquito room. By placing gauze on the wall of the house I had prevented this, and I used to enjoy sitting in that room watching the various kinds of mosquitoes and other creeping, crawling, and flying pests vainly endeavouring to reach me.

One evening, as I was lying on my long chair after dinner with a cup of black coffee and a glass of green crème de menthe, I saw, slowly crawling up the side of the house, a large red centipede. It was about five inches long and as thick as my little finger. I thrilled with joy when I noticed that he was in between the copper gauze and the wall so that he could not possibly escape as I squashed him flat by pressing the gauze against the wall. But to my horror, as I squashed him he began to glow like phosphorus in the dark and the juices of his body corroded the metal gauze so badly that eventually a piece of it dropped out and the dead centipede fell into the mosquito room.

Lots of the jungle insects are phosphorescent and so are some of the caterpillars. In fact, I have actually seen trees that were distinctly phosphorescent, but I regret that my knowledge of botany does not permit my giving the tree's scientific name.

When I had first arrived in Kedah, Hussein, who was still with me, secured a faithful Malay servant for me called Ismail. He was a Kedah Malay, the kind of faithful soul one reads about in books. He stayed with me for two years.

Soon after we went to Terap, I noticed Ismail placing little white flags around the house and on the edge of the jungle. When I asked him about it, he said: "This place is haunted; there are many evil spirits here, sir!"

I laughed at him, but he was serious about it and repeated his warning. The Malays and the Siamese who came to visit us either out of curiosity or to sell chickens used to say in wonderment: "Fancy building a house in Terap! Aren't you afraid of ghosts?" When I laughed and said "no," they answered "Ah! Look out, sir, this is a terrible place; that is why no Malays live here!"

Soon we all began to feel horribly creepy, but I discovered that Luard was the innocent cause of the epidemic because she had placed under the house six setting hens, and our dining room was swarming with chicken lice. Each hen hatched out about a dozen or more little chickens, but as soon as the fond mothers took their babies out for a walk huge hawks came along and stole the chicks. Rarely does a Malay hen rear more than one chick, because of hawks; but the hens are fatalists, and whenever a hen sees a hawk coming, she picks out her nicest chick and promptly sits on it, while the others scatter about and are carried off and slain.

We had nearly two hundred chickens and several ducks when we went to Terap, but the place certainly had a "hoodoo." First of all, the ducks died, except the old drake, then the drake went mad and used to eat more little chicks than the hawks. Then the chickens began walking about with their mouths wide open and died by the dozen. At last we picked out about twenty good white Leghorns and the same number of black Minorcas, all of them fine healthy birds, and kept them away from the other fowls in their own special fowl house. One morning, when Luard went to let them out, all the white ones had disappeared and in the corner of the house was a huge python. The snake had entered at night through a small hole about six inches in diameter, and eaten all the white chickens, presumably because he couldn't see the black ones; then having twenty large lumps all along his body, which prevented him from going out the way he came in, he had curled up and gone to sleep. We put him in a sack without any difficulty and sold him to a Chinaman who said he wanted him for *obat* (medicine).

Our next misfortune was to lose our faithful old cook, Salleh, who got fever so badly that I had to let him leave and return to his home, taking the Tukan Ayer with him. In his place I secured an Indian cook called Govinden, who was bitten on the instep by a centipede the same day he arrived at Terap and died shortly after in the hospital. I then got another Indian cook, called Tambapillai, who brought his wife and little boy with him. A few hours after he arrived he came into our room and asked me to give him ten dollars because his wife wanted to offer up a sacrifice of a live goat in order to propitiate the evil spirits. When I objected to the ten-dollar part of the sacrifice, he said that two dollars' worth of watermelons would have the same effect, and I gave him the money.

That evening his wife started business. She seemed to be in a trance and wandered about the house and the garden with her husband following her, his arms full of watermelons. Every now and then she started back, as if she had seen a ghost, whereupon the cook seized a watermelon and cut it in half with a large knife, leaving the two halves on the ground.   By the time she had finished "devil dodging," we had watermelons in bed and watermelons under the chairs, in the cupboards, in the fowl house, down the well, and in numerous other places.

For several weeks after this performance we had no more fever or misfortune, and even the old drake stopped eating the chickens, so that I considered the two dollars well spent.

A few weeks after we settled down at Terap, an old Chinaman built a house and started a pig farm about a quarter of a mile from our house.   Fortunately there was dense jungle between us and the Chinaman, so that we were not bothered by his pigs. Living with him were his wife, his mother-in-law, and two children about twelve years old, a boy and girl.

Just before the Chinese New Year I was out inspecting some work and met the man and his wife on their way to Kulim, where they were going to purchase food and firecrackers for their New Year celebration.   They left the house in charge of the mother-in-law.   On my way home the next day when I reached the pig farm all that was left of it was a heap of smouldering embers.   About twenty yards from the house was the body of the mother-in-law, burnt to a crisp.   While I was looking at the tragic sight, the father and mother returned from their shopping expedition.   The woman immediately began looking for her children and soon found the remains of her little daughter but no sign of her son. She then sat down in the ruins of her house and began the most terrible wailing I have ever heard, tearing her clothes to pieces and throwing ashes over her head. While she was doing this, we heard a rustle in the bushes, and out came the little Chinese boy, very frightened and badly burned about his neck and head. His mother went into raptures of joy at seeing him, but as the father continued raking over the ashes and moaning to himself, I thought I would comfort him. "Now, there is no use to cry any more. Hadn't we better dig a grave and bury your daughter and mother-in-law?" I said gently. The man looked up reproachfully: "They don't matter, sir," he said; "it's my pigs I am grieving for!"

In fact, he wouldn't lift a finger to bury them, and as there was no one else to do so, Luard and I rolled the bodies in a sheet and buried them ourselves.

Terap certainly seemed to be under some kind of a curse, and the next occurrence was extremely uncanny.

We had a dog called Peter, and one day, about eleven o'clock in the morning, he began a mournful howling, with his nose stuck straight up into the air. Ismail exclaimed: "*Orang suda mati!* [Someone is dead!]"—and that same afternoon a Chinese tin miner came to the house and reported that his partner was lying dead in a house a mile away. I said: "When did he die?" And he replied: "At 11 o'clock this morning!"

A few days afterward, to my astonishment, there arrived at my bungalow two strange Englishmen, obviously dressed in tropical clothes for the first time in their lives. One was tall and clean-shaven; the other was short and had a long, drooping moustache. They introduced themselves as brothers, and gave their name as Thompson. They said that they had just arrived from Lancashire, England, and were looking for some nice jungle to buy and convert into a rubber estate. I gave them a good deal of help and eventually they acquired some of the jungle close to Terap, built a bungalow there, and within a year the short brother was dead. Cheerful place, Terap! Just after Thompson died, I was surveying a river crossing for a bridge site when something bit me on the ankle, just above the top of my boot. When I got home that afternoon and took off my boot my foot began to swell, and in a few hours it was about twice its normal size and I was in agony. There was no doubt that I had been bitten by a poisonous snake, because not only did I notice the two small punctures in the skin that day, but I still have the marks on my ankle at the time of writing. For over a week

Luard nursed me, applying hot fomentations to my leg. I had, of course, applied the usual snake-bite remedy, rubbing crystals of permanganate into cuts made in the bite with a razor. At the end of a week I had a hole in my leg big enough to hold an egg, and it was three weeks before I could walk, and months before the wound healed. For nearly a month I used to be carried about to inspect my work by four sturdy Chinese coolies.

The nearest escape from a tragedy in the family was one morning when Luard met a king cobra face to face. She was coming from the bathroom, which was built some distance away from the house, when she was startled to see, reared up in the middle of the pathway with its hood expanded, a large hamadryad. As she stopped, the snake darted at her ankles. She sprang back and walked backward to the bathroom with the snake following her. There she snatched up an old broom handle with which she kept the snake at bay, knocking its head to one side every time it struck at her legs. Her shouts attracted the attention of Ismail, who rushed up with a heavy stick and attacked the snake in the rear, killing it. It was about six feet long and dark olive-green in colour. Ismail told us that he had killed another snake like it that same morning, and that no doubt this was the mate looking for revenge.

The king cobra is the largest and most dangerous poisonous snake in the world. It is said to grow to a length of eighteen feet and is the only snake that will attack and even follow a man.

My next misfortune was to develop colitis. I got thinner and thinner and so ill that I certainly thought I was going to die. I consulted a doctor in Penang named Sharp, who treated me for about two months.

While I was ill Luard was carried out of Terap suffering from malaria and dengue, and eventually, after living in the jungle for several years and enduring all kinds of hardship with a spice of adventure, she sailed for America to recuperate and three months later I joined her.

"Do you ever want to go back?"

I have heard the question dozens of times and there is always the same answer.

Both my wife and I are longing to return; we loved the life, we liked the Malays, but we failed to appreciate, until too late, the wonderful opportunity that we had for research work, purely *causa scientiæ*.

I am counting the days until I can return to Mysterious Malaya, but I do not want to live there for ever, thank you! You hear the call of good Old Broadway and Piccadilly just as strongly in the Jungle as after a few months in New York or London you hear there the call of the East.

APPENDIX

The information contained in this appendix has
been compiled by the Federated Malay States
Government, and is used in this volume by their
kind permission.

APPENDIX

FAUNA

The fauna of British Malaya are excelled in number of species only in parts of South America.

Elephants were once numerous, except on the islands of Singapore and Penang. The opening up of the country for rubber cultivation has much restricted their range, though even within a few miles of Kuala Lumpur damage is still done to plantations. The local elephant is not large, even when compared with other Asiatic races, and big tuskers are very rare— it is doubtful if any specimen with tusks heavier than a hundred pounds has been obtained. The Malayan elephant, however, has been persecuted for its ivory, and under existing legislation no male whose tusks appear to be less than thirty pounds in weight may be shot. Two species of rhinoceros are known. The smaller two-horned species at one time formed an article of export from the Dindings. Of the one-horned Javan variety only three or four individuals from the southern districts of Perak are extant in collections. It appears to be dying out. Like the elephant, the rhinoceros is much persecuted, as its horn and almost every portion of its anatomy command large prices from Chinese medicine dealers. More numerous is the Malayan tapir, a parti-coloured beast of ancient lineage. It possesses no trophies of sporting or commercial value, and so long as suitable forest remains unfelled it is not likely to diminish in numbers. The *seladang* or Malayan bison is almost identical with the Indian. It is now almost extinct in Selangor, rare in Perak, but fairly abundant in certain districts of Negri Sembilan and Pahang. It is met with in the Unfederated Malay States in diminished numbers, but no longer exists in the Colony. Deer of several species, *rusa*, the sambur of India, *kijang*, the barking deer and two forms of mouse deer, dainty animals hardly heavier than a hare, are common. The serow or goat antelope occurs in fair numbers in remote or almost untraversable localities. The Malayan tiger cannot compare in size with the Indian or Chinese beast. A small bear does much damage to coconut plantations. Wild dogs are rare and local. The jackal is unknown. Monkeys range in size from the *siamang*, a large anthropoid ape, and the *brok* (used for picking coconuts) to the long-tailed *lotong* and *kra* and the tailless *slow loris*, a thick-furred little beast of nocturnal habits. Malaya is the metropolis of the squirrels. They range from an animal bigger than a cat to one little larger than a small rat. Rats are numerous and varied and are a serious agricultural pest. The Norway rat, the chief carrier of plague, is only just beginning to obtain a footing in the larger seaports. Over sixty species of bats are listed. They include the flying fox, or *keluang*, the largest of the order, with a spread of the wing of nearly five feet, which may be seen in millions amongst the mangroves of the coast. A species, which in weight, if not in size, claims to be considered the smallest existing mammal, is also a Malayan animal. Whales are only casual visitors, specimens of the lesser Indian fin whale, and possibly of the sperm whale, having been occasionally stranded on Malaya's shores. Dolphins and porpoises are common. Seals are unknown.

About seven hundred species of birds are on record. Some forty game birds and pigeons occur, the former including the argus and several other species of pheasants, the peafowl, and two small quail. From the difficult nature of their habitat these birds do not appeal to the sportsman. Pigeon afford good sport. They exist in great variety, and are distributed over the more open parts of the country. Certain forms, notably the large black and white pied imperial pigeon, are found only near salt water. The snipe-shooting is almost the best in the world, and for those who will brave the mud, there is good shore shooting at certain seasons, for such birds as curlew, whimbrel, greenshank, and redshank. Ducks, except the tree duck in a few localities, are hardly known, and do not frequent the mud-flats. Parrots are scarce, both in variety and in number. Kingfishers of brilliant plumage are numerous, and so are bee-eaters, barbets, trogons, and a lot of smaller species of interest only to the bird-lover. Especially characteristic are the hornbills, large birds of clumsy and laboured flight, remarkable for the bizarre form of the head.

Though reptiles of all groups are very common they do not obtrude themselves as they do in India and tropical Australia. Crocodiles are numerous, especially on the lower reaches of the rivers debouching on the Straits of Malacca, and they take a larger toll of human life than any other wild animal. Specimens nearly thirty feet long are recorded, but those exceeding sixteen feet are exceptional. Another but harmless form, allied to the ghavial of India, is found in small numbers. Most of the poisonous snakes known in India, excluding Russell's viper, are found, but many are rare. The hamadryad or king cobra, the largest of all venomous snakes, recorded as attaining a length of eighteen feet six inches, is frequently met with, and black cobras are common; but few deaths from snake-bite occur, and those are due mostly to sea-snakes. Lizards are very common. Most familiar are the little geckoes or *chichak*, which eat insects at night in every house, and the large *Varanus*, erroneously known as the monitor lizard. The flying lizard with brilliantly coloured throat and brightly striped wing membranes is a denizen of every coconut grove. Turtles and tortoises are found in great variety, the marine forms including the edible turtle and that from which tortoise-shell is derived. The rivers and ponds harbour several soft-billed forms, while many box tortoises inhabit the jungle.

The rivers, where they have not been fouled by mining silt, are inhabited by large numbers of fish, probably of not less than three hundred species. They vary in size from large catfish and carp, allied to the *mahseer* and *tor* of India, to little puddle-frequenting forms, under half an inch long, which find their relatives amongst the "millions" of Barbados, much extolled at one time as mosquito-killers. Sea fish of course are even more varied, but present no features differentiating them from those inhabiting other Indian seas of the same depth and within the same parallels. In suitable localities both fresh-water fish and sea fish would afford good sport, for example near Singapore, in the Dindings, and on the

East Coast of the Peninsula. In the interior the middle reaches of the Tembeling River in Pahang abound in large fish.

Competent authorities estimate that not less than a quarter of a million species of insects exist in Malaya. Of these the immense majority are minute and remain to be described. Among the larger forms more than a thousand butterflies are known, ranging from the lordly emerald and black *Ornithoptera brookeana* to minute "blues" and "skippers." Moths are equally varied and include the giant Atlas moth; and so are beetles, which include massive forms several ounces in weight.

FLORA

The flora of British Malaya are most closely related to that of the adjacent parts of the Malay Archipelago, which are near the Equator, and somewhat less closely to that of Siam and Indo-China to the north. They are characterized by very great wealth in number of forms.

Most people who have not visited the tropics imagine large numbers of palms, vivid masses of colour and dense growth forming the "impenetrable jungle" of travellers' tales. Closer acquaintance shows the incorrectness of these impressions. Palms there are many, but they are usually overshadowed by larger forms, and it is seldom that they are the dominating feature in the landscape. The palm most often noticed is the coconut palm, which is introduced and is seen only in cultivation.

Bright flowers and plants with brightly coloured leaves abound, but their brilliance is less striking than most people anticipate because it is found in less extensive masses than is the case at certain seasons in temperate climates. The number of brilliantly coloured plants found at any time in the tropics is much greater than at any time in the cold climates, but the mass of green foliage of other plants is so limitless that most casual observers comment on the lack of colour in Malayan forests.

"Impenetrable jungle" is a figment of the popular imagination. Jungle is often dense, but generally it can be penetrated with little effort and a small amount of cutting. It is thickest where the original forest has been felled and secondary growth of low-growing trees, shrubs, and climbers has intruded. In general, high forest of good quality is easy to walk through, and often no cutting is needed to clear the way.

As in many parts of the world, the vegetation of the settled areas is different from the original cover, and it is necessary to get away from the larger settlements to find what the characteristic vegetation of the country is like.

The whole country was once covered by forest, and one of the most marked features of the flora is the preponderance of woody forms. The Malay Peninsula contains more species of trees than are known from all of British India and Burma. It is probable that there are more than three thousand species of trees, as compared with less than six hundred in the whole of the British Isles.

There are no large areas of bamboo forest such as occur in India, Burma, and Siam. This is probably because there is no prolonged dry season as in those countries.

The original forest is a fine example of what a tropical forest can be. The average height of the largest trees is at least one hundred fifty feet, and many of them are a hundred feet to the first branch.

Whenever any forested area is cleared, the ground is quickly covered with new growth, of different character from the original cover. Various quick-growing plants rush in and occupy the area. Many of the short-lived plants show extraordinarily rapid growth, at any rate, for a time. The plants of larger growth usually grow at a slower rate, which may, however, be rapid in comparison with growth in colder climates. Some large trees grow in girth more than one and a half inches a year, but many of the trees have slower rates, and some of them are very slow indeed. Some of the plants of the lowland forests are obviously very old and there are comparatively few of the large trees that reach their full size in one hundred years. Many trees which have to endure shading when young may remain almost stationary for very many years or until some fortuitous chance lets in the light and gives them scope to accomplish the rate of growth of which they are capable.

The plants most characteristic of British Malaya are: the large timber trees belonging to the family *Dipterocarpaceæ*, the climbing palms which are known as rattans, and the orchids, ferns, and other epiphytes which are found so abundantly upon the trees.

FORESTS

The commercial forests of British Malaya, British North Borneo, and Sarawak occupy an area of approximately seventy thousand square miles, of which more than half is in the island of Borneo. They are all near the Equator and extend from about one degree to about seven degrees north. In the eastern tropics it seems that the closer one approaches the Equator, the more complex in number of species is the composition of the forest. Thus, the Malay Peninsula has something like twenty-five hundred species of trees recorded as occurring within its bounds; and it is very probable that when we know the forest better we shall find that the actual number of tree species is more than three thousand. The forests of Borneo are also very rich in tree species, and it is probable that the total number in British Malaya, British North Borneo, and Sarawak is considerably in excess of four thousand. It is not uncommon to find more than a hundred species of trees on a single acre.

Although the number of tree species is so very great, the proportion of species which are of economic importance is relatively small. Most writers who have dealt with tropical forests have strongly emphasized their extreme complexity, and it is only within the past generation that studies by foresters have shown that, in spite of the great number of species, the greatest part of the volume of timber produced comes from but a few, often closely related forms. Very often 60 per cent. to 80 per cent. or more of the volume of timber produced by a given area will be the product of no more than four or five species. There is essential similarity in the forests of the whole region. The same kinds of trees are found to make up the bulk of the forest in all the countries, although there are specific differences and each country may have forms peculiar to it. Commercially the woods and other products of the forest are of very much the same nature throughout the region.

One family of plants, the *Dipterocarpaceæ*, makes up most of the volume of the forest throughout the whole region, supplying more than 60 per cent. by volume of all the commercial timber. The trees of this family form the top story of the forest. Underneath them is the second story made up of trees of a slightly smaller size, spreading out their crowns on a slightly lower level. Underneath these there are one or more stories composed of small or medium-sized trees which can stand a good deal of shade and which do not form very large trunks. Below these there is still another stratum or story containing the plants which remain near ground level. The lowest stories of the forest contain great numbers of species but produce a very small amount of timber.

The undergrowth is often very dense, although areas which can fairly be called impenetrable jungle are rarely, if ever, found.

In general, the better the yield of timber, the less dense is the undergrowth, and in some of the best forests one can walk through without the necessity of doing much cutting of undergrowth out of the way. The constant high humidity causes the forests to be nearly always moist and it is rarely that fires can do any serious damage. In some places, where the drainage is poor, there are large fresh-water swamps. Some of these are quite extensive, and it is probable that, collectively, they occupy as much as 10 per cent. of the land surface of the Malay Peninsula. These swamps may contain certain amounts of good timber, but they are not suited to the requirements of many of our best trees, and the yield of timber from them is usually very poor. In some of these places there is an accumulation of peaty soil to a depth of some feet.

The better classes of forest are on well-drained soil and extend from sea level up to about two thousand feet. There are considerable areas of forest above two thousand feet, but these mountain forests are not at present of commercial importance because of the small size of trees which they contain and because of the cost of extracting material from them. Besides, most of them need to be preserved for the protection of stream flow and for the prevention of erosion. Trees will stand on steeper slopes here than is usually the case elsewhere. The average gradient of slope on the hills of the higher country is very steep.

All of the commercial timbers of British Malaya are of a class of wood which would be called hardwood in a temperate climate. The soft woods or conifers are not represented in commercial quantity or are inaccessible because of their occurrence at high elevation. The most abundant woods of the region are light in weight and are soft, and are known by the names Meranti and Seraya. Some of them have great natural beauty and are suitable for use in ornamental work. The very hard and heavy woods of great durability are produced in quantities sufficient for local use, but very few of them are in sufficient quantity to be available for export purposes.

There is a very large industrial use of wood in parts of the Malay Peninsula, and it is probable that most of the species from the Malay Peninsula will be needed in the future for local use. There will be a certain amount available for export from some of the Unfederated Malay States. The principal supplies of export wood are to be found in Borneo. In British North Borneo there are timber companies at work which are already doing an export trade. There is also opportunity for the development of an export trade from Sarawak in the future.

Throughout the region the forest products other than timber, which are known as minor forest products, are of great importance. The principal of these are *rotan*, produced by various climbing palms, *damar*, which is a resin that is produced by various trees principally of the family *Dipterocarpaceæ*, gutta percha, and cutch. All of these countries produce *rotan*, *damar*, and gutta percha, and the Bornean countries produce considerable quantities of cutch. The *rotans* are known only from the eastern tropics and reach their highest development in the Malay region. The *damars* of the *Dipterocarpaceæ* also reach their highest development in the same region. Gutta percha of best quality is produced only in a limited portion of the Malayan region.

Details about the amounts of forest products available in the different countries and the regulations for the working of such products can be obtained by application to the

Conservator of Forests, F. M. S. & S. S., Kuala Lumpur.
Conservator of Forests, Sandakan, B. N. B.
Conservator of Forests, Kuching, Sarawak.

AGRICULTURE

Before the coming of Europeans to Malaya, agriculture was limited to the production of the immediate necessities of the cultivator, and it is possible that the aboriginal inhabitants grew no crops at all but relied on indigenous edible roots and fruits for food. The Malays introduced rice cultivation from Sumatra and the planting of fruit trees in and around villages.

The Portuguese and the Dutch from the 15th Century onward interested themselves in the production of spices, and large tracts of grass land around Malacca bear witness to their labours. Nutmegs also were cultivated to a considerable extent around Penang.

Later, Chinese immigrants understood the cultivation of tapioca, gambier, pepper, and pineapples, especially in Singapore and Johore.

Of all these crops, tapioca alone is still grown on a fairly large scale, while attempts are now being made to revive the pineapple industry. All suffered, at different times, from inability to cope with falling markets, probably because of poor labour supply, and impoverishment of soil due to lack of manure resulting from scarcity of farm animals.

After the advent of British Administration, British and other capital started to come into the Peninsula; and coffee, sugar, and coconut plantations were established, coffee chiefly in Selangor, sugar and coconuts on the low-lying coastal areas of Province Wellesley and Perak.

Coffee cultivation never became extensive, and after some time the plantations found themselves in grave difficulties from the fall in price of their product and also from disease. At this critical time attention was directed to Para rubber and progress with that cultivation has continued steadily ever since, to the complete elimination of the coffee and sugar industries, Malaya having proved to be suited in an extraordinary degree to the requirements of *Hevea brasiliensis*. These requirements are: a hot humid climate, fairly heavy and equally distributed rainfall, and the absence of strong winds, as the tree is structurally weak. Further, the labour required on rubber plantations is small in proportion to the value of the crop collected, an essential for success when reliance has to be placed on expensive imported labour.

The extension of rubber cultivation went forward without check until the catastrophic fall in the market price of the commodity in 1920, brought about by over-production relative to the consuming capacity of an impoverished world. This slump was the more severe in that rubber was almost the only essential commodity which had not soared in price during the war.

At present a scheme to restrict exports by imposing prohibitive rates of export duty on every pound of rubber exported by producers in excess of a standard allowance is in force and has done much to ameliorate the disastrous condition in which the majority of estates found themselves, of having further to depress the market by producing at full capacity to obtain ready money with which to pay and keep together immigrant labour forces. Once dispersed and re-patriated, labour would have been extremely difficult to replace. The slump was equally hard on native holders, who had in the past been quick to see the advantages of rubber as a crop and had cut out fruit trees and abandoned paddy areas to devote themselves to rubber growing.

In view of the large returns given by rubber, it is not surprising that the area under coconuts has in-creased only slightly in recent years. Much of the alluvial land, on which coconuts thrive best, has been planted with rubber; and, on the whole, coconut estates do not receive as much cultivation and at-tention as they deserve. Consequently, big dividends are rare despite the increasing demand for vegetable oils and a fair average price for copra (the kernel dried for export). There is a small export of desiccated coconut to supply the demand of confectioners.

Probably one third of the area devoted to coconut cultivation is native owned.

Rice cultivation does not lend itself to capitalistic ventures, and is essentially a matter for small holders —almost invariably Malays.

Rice is of two kinds, wet and dry, the former growing only on land which can be flooded for part of the planting season. Wet-rice areas are naturally river valleys, and have been in recent years considerably extended by the adoption of artificial irrigation.

The Krian Irrigation Scheme, which has been in operation for more than twenty years, supplies water to 55,000 acres in one block in North Perak, this being the largest area artificially irrigated. The success of this scheme is reflected in a settled population, thanks to an assured food supply, so that Krian is now the most prosperous agricultural district in Malaya.

The Titi Serong Rice Experiment Station, situated in Krian, is one of the chief concerns of the Department of Agriculture. Considerable headway has been made at this station in selecting heavy-yielding strains of paddy, and supplies of selected seed have been issued to test stations scattered over the country for trial before distribution to cultivators.

Dry paddy is grown like any other cereal, often on

hill slopes, but the area under this form of cultivation aggregates only 43,000 acres.

Many varieties of fruit trees are cultivated, and near the towns there is considerable activity in market-gardening, but no crop other than rubber, rice, and coconuts can be regarded as a serious contribution to Malayan agriculture.

The importance of agriculture to Malaya has been recognized by Government in many ways, not the least of which is the upkeep of the Department of Agriculture. Starting in 1906 with a modest staff of four Europeans, this department has steadily grown in size and scope to a present European staff of thirty-four and many assistants, chiefly educated Malays. The results of experimental work and other matters of interest are published monthly in numbers of the Malayan *Agricultural Journal*.

The Department has, naturally, devoted most attention to rubber and paddy, but a steady search for other crops is always in progress. For instance, it has recently been shown that cotton can be grown with a fair degree of success provided that pest control is systematized, though it has not yet been tested on a commercial scale. Several other crops, e. g., roselle fibre, show promise for cultivation on a comparatively small scale as adjuncts to rubber, but the African oil palm is the only new crop which, so far,

has given satisfactory results as a large-scale invest-
ment.

STATISTICS

Approximate area under rubber in 1922......2,225,000 acres
      "   "   " coconuts " "   .... 250,000 "
      "   "   " paddy " "   ..... 669,000 "
Approximate net export of Plantation rubber
     in 1922............................... 213,000 tons
Approximate net export of copra in 1922...... 104,495 "
      "   "   " "paddy " " 135,000,000 gantangs*
Value of net exports of rubber in 1922. ....£16,531,819
   " " "   "   " copra " "............. 2,262,508

  *1 gantang = 1 gallon.

MINING

Malaya is renowned for the quantity and quality of its tin. Roughly, thirty-five thousand tons of tin are won yearly in the Federated Malay States. "Straits" tin is capable of exceptional fluidity, and so can cover steel plates, such as are used for all purposes of canning, with a thinner film than tin from elsewhere.

There were tin mines in the Peninsula at least as early as the 15th Century A. D.

The ore occurs in granite, quartzite, shales, phyllites, schists, and limestone, and in detrital deposits and soil derived from these rocks. Its occurrence is patchy, so that there are more or less well-defined tin-fields. The concentrates of tin ore from the mines are in the form of sand, in which good crystals are rare. In the limestone of Kinta cassiterite occurs in pipes and veins, and is associated generally with large quantities of metallic sulphides, particularly arseno-pyrite.

Tin ore was and is still concentrated by making a stream of water wash away the lighter minerals. Ground-sluicing of the foothills and open-cast mining on the flats were the old-fashioned Chinese methods of recovering the ore. Narrow shafts, too, were dug, where there was a thick cover of worthless ground. Exhaustion of the richer deposits and improvement in machinery led to scientific innovations. In 1904 there were 192,669 mining coolies and machinery of 6,539 horse power; in 1922 there were only 82,195 coolies and machinery of 59,278 horse power. Puddlers, steam pumps, and monitors were introduced, then electro-magnetic separators for removing impurities (including monazite) from the ore, then floating barges and dredges. Bucket dredging has come in since 1910; to-day there are 41 such dredges at work, 5 being built and several more contemplated; most are worked by steam, but a few by electricity; the largest can cut 120,000 yards a month. More recent still is the suction cutter. Water power is used to a great extent, both directly for monitors and hydraulic elevators and indirectly for the generation of electric power. Machinery of all kinds is used, from the simple portable boiler and engine of 12 horse power to large steam electric plants of 2,000 horse power. Suction, gas, diesel and semi-diesel, oil and petrol engines are employed.

About 250,000 tons of coal are won yearly from a mine in Selangor. Underground and open-cast methods are used.

Iron ore of very good quality is being exported from Johore by a Japanese company at the rate of 10,000 tons monthly.

Gold is found in small quantities, chiefly along a broad belt extending northward from near Mount Ophir into the west of Kelantan. It is found, also, outside this belt, and about a thousand ounces are recovered yearly from alluvial tin ore in Perak. The Raub Australian Gold Mining Company wins some 14,600 ounces per annum from low-grade ore in calcareous shale.

Tungsten ores, in the form of wolfram and scheelite, are found in fairly large quantities.

COMMERCE

The inhabitants of British Malaya were recorded as 3,358,054 at the last census. The wealth of this small community may be inferred from the country's contributions to the World War. The colony contributed in local war loans, in investments, in imperial loans, and in gifts, just under £15,500,000, the Federated Malay States just under £13,500,000, and the Malay States outside the Federation £85,000. For the Malayan Air Squadron and the various war funds and charities £750,000 was raised by private subscriptions from members of every race—British, Malay, Chinese, Indian, Eurasian, Japanese, Arab, Jew. Before the war the rulers of the Federated Malay States had arranged to present to the British Navy the battleship H. M. S. *Malaya*, which took part in the fight off Jutland. Toward the end of 1922 the assets of the colony exceeded its liabilities by £6,700,000. The Federated Malay States has built railways at a cost of some £20,000,000 out of current revenue.

Tin and rubber are mainly responsible for the prosperity of the Malay States. In the Straits Settlements also there are agricultural interests, but their

largest asset is trade, particularly that of the great
free port of Singapore, where duties are levied only on
alcohol, tobacco, and petroleum.   In addition to native craft and local ships, it is visited by fifty lines of
ocean-going steamers.   The total tonnage of merchant
vessels arriving and departing in 1922 at the ports of
the colony was just under 27,000,000 tons.

Midway between Suez and Japan, between India
and China, it is a great coaling station and one of the
world's biggest centres for the distribution of oil and
oil fuel.

The trade of Singapore is made up of direct exports
of home production and of re-exports of articles from
neighbouring countries, which are handled, refined,
and graded before re-shipment.   The trade in certain
articles of the latter class is enormous.   Nearly all
the tin ore of Malaya and much from other countries
is smelted there.   In 1920 rubber to the value of
more than £31,000,000, and in 1921 and in 1922
(when there was a slump) rubber worth just under
£11,000,000 and just under £16,000,000 respectively
was exported from the colony.

The imports into the colony for 1922 were valued
at £66,692,000 and the exports at £62,060,000 and
the aggregate trade for the year, excluding interset-
tlement trade, was £128.7 millions.   The chief exports are rubber, tin, rice, copra, salted fish, pepper,

preserved pineapples, rattans. In 1922 goods to the value of £7,386,000 were imported from and goods to the value of £4,799,000 were exported to the United Kingdom; goods to the value of £1,892,000 were imported from the United States of America and goods to the value of £20,750,000 were exported thither. The huge export trade to the United States of America consists mainly of rubber and tin.

Through the ports of the Straits Settlements most of the products of the Malay States are exported. In 1922 the aggregate trade of the Federated Malay States, excluding bullion and specie, was £25.5 and in 1921 £27.8 millions, the drop being due to the fall in the *values* (but not the *quantities*) of imports. The distribution of trade in imports and exports was approximately as follows: Singapore 41 and 40 per cent.; Penang 22 and 39 per cent.; the United Kingdom 15 and 8 per cent.; British Colonies 9 and 11 per cent., and the remainder to foreign countries.

Most of the import trade of Malaya is with countries within the Empire.

ARTS AND CRAFTS

Malay arts and crafts have suffered from the novel attraction of Western wares, the competition of Chinese craftsmen, the passing of a particular type of civilization with its appurtenances, the introduction of aniline dyes. In the old days every court had its maker of weapons, its worker in silver and gold, its weavers and women skilled in embroidery. To-day the Malay rajah wears a kris only on ceremonial occasions and that a weapon which is an heirloom. With the decay of betel-chewing the use of elaborate betel sets has died out and European cigarette cases have taken their place. Even the *sarong*, the Malay's national "kilt," is giving way in towns to khaki trousers and most of these still worn come from Manchester and India.

The finest materials in the world for basket-work are found in the forests of the Malayan region. The best baskets are made in Malacca, but as it takes at least a month to make a fine set, their manufacture is of dilettante rather than commercial interest.

Some graceful but primitive pottery is made in Perak and Pahang.

Weaving in the Western States of the Peninsula came, like the Malays, from Sumatra. The tie-and-die work of the Malays and the use of gold and silver thread can be traced to Indian models. Selangor is noted for polished or calendered cloths impressed with gold-leaf by means of carved wooden stamps. The striped and plaid cloths of Kelantan are distinctive. The beautiful tie-and-dye silks of Trengganu are no longer woven owing to the meretricious attraction of bright aniline dyes.

Most Malay work in brass, silver, and gold bears traces of Indian influence. But Mohammedanism has saved the Malay from the crude realism of much Indian art. Perak, more than any other State, has a style of its own for silverware, and this style is well illustrated in Swettenham's "British Malaya" and Ling Roth's "Oriental Silverwork." Chinese influence on Malay metal-work has been slight. Old European influence may be detected in watch-shaped caskets, in hinges, and in saucer and plate shapes. Filigree-work jewellery is still made in Negri Sembilan, but most modern Malay jewellery is the handiwork of Chinese smiths. The most elaborate of all Peninsular metal-work is a kind of niello, till recently made in Kedah and in Siamese

Malaya, on a silver ground with the hollows of the pattern a black sulphide, and the high relief gilded.

The "accursed Malayan creese [kris]" interests the schoolboy, the ethnographist, the collector of weapons. Some have thought that its wavy sinister blade was modelled originally on the horns of an animal; others ascribe its invention to primitive snake-worshippers. The hilt known to Malays as "the fevered Javanese" is said to represent the Garuda or fabulous animal whereon Vishnu rides, though the attitude of the figure is also that of an Indonesian demon. These weapons are valued for age, bloodstains, and, above all, lucky marks in the damascene of the blades. The latest theory finds in the Javanese kris only five basic patterns of damascene named after plants, as also five basic plant motifs in the batik fabrics of Java, and suggests that Javanese folklore points to five plants having been originally the totems of five clans. A long straight kris was used for executions in Malay times, the blade being pressed from shoulder to heart. A slightly curved dagger known as the "pepper-crusher" is another typical Malay weapon. The sword was introduced.

Some fine Malay embroidery of gold thread on silk and velvet backgrounds is done at courts like Kuala Kangsar. Pillows, mats, and slippers are favourite articles.   Chinese and Indian influences can be detected.

In the Peninsula, Negri Sembilan especially is noted for wood-carving bearing foliated patterns.

A little lace (with a Portuguese name) is made in Malacca.

BIBLIOGRAPHY OF MODERN BOOKS
RELATING TO MALAYA

GENERAL

ANNANDALE, NELSON & H. C. ROBINSON. Fasciculi Malayenses. London, 1903.

BLAGDEN, C. O. *See* SKEAT, W. W.

BLAND, R. N. Historical Tombstones of Malacca. 1905. ill. [Elliot Stock, London.]

BOULGER, DEMETRIUS C. Life of Sir Stamford Raffles. 1897. [Horace Marshall & Son, London.]

BUCKLEY, CHARLES B. Anecdotal History of Old Times in Singapore. 1902. ill. [Fraser & Neave Ltd., Singapore.]

CHERRY, W. T. Geography of British Malaya. 1923. 4th ed. [M. P. H., Singapore.]

CLIFFORD, SIR HUGH. Bush-whacking and Other Sketches, 1901. [W. Blackwood & Sons, London.] In a Corner of Asia. 1899. [T. Fisher Unwin, London.] In Court and Kampong. 1897. [Grant Richards, London.] Malayan Monochromes. 1913. [J. Murray, London.] Sally: a Study. 1904. [W. Blackwood & Sons, London.] Saleh: a Sequel. 1908. [W. Blackwood & Sons, London.] Since the Beginning. 1898. [Grant Richards, London.] Studies in Brown Humanity. 1898. [Grant Richards, London.]

COOK, J. A. B. Sunny Singapore, 1907. [Elliot Stock, London.]

EVANS, IVOR H. N. Studies in Religion, Folklore, and Custom in British North Borneo and the Malay Peninsula. 1923. [Cambridge University Press.]

FRANKAU, GILBERT. "Tid'apa." 1921. [Chatto & Windus, London.]

GIMLETTE, JOHN D. Malay Poisons and Charm Cures. 1923. 2d ed. [J. & A. Churchill, London.]

GRAHAM, W. A. Kelantan: a State of the Malay Peninsula. 1908. ill. [J. Maclehose & Sons, Glasgow.]

HALE, A. Adventures of John Smith in Malaya. 1909. [E. J. Brill, Leyden.]

HARRISON, CUTHBERT W. An Illustrated Guide to the Federated Malay States. 1923. ill. [Malay States Information Agency, London.] The Magic of Malaya. [John Lane, London.]

HUBBACK, T. R. Three Months in Pahang in

Search of Big Game. n. d. [Kelly & Walsh, Ltd., Singapore.]

MAKEPEACE, W. M. and OTHERS. One Hundred Years of Singapore. 1923. [J. Murray, London.]

MAXWELL, GEORGE. In Malay Forests. 1907. [W. Blackwood & Sons, London.]

MAXWELL, C. N. Malayan Fishes, 1922. ill. [M. P. H., Singapore.]

MAYER, CHARLES. Trapping Wild Animals in Malay Jungles. 1922. [T. Fisher Unwin, London.]

RIDLEY. H. N. Flora of the Malay Peninsula. Vol 1, 1908. [M. P. H., Singapore.] Vol. 2, 1923. [L. Reeve & Co., London.]

ROTH, H. LING. Oriental Silverwork—Malay and Chinese. 1910. [Truslove & Hanson Ltd., London.]

SKEAT, W. W. Fables and Folk-tales from an Eastern Forest. 1901. [Cambridge University Press.]

Malay Magic. 1900. ill. [Macmillan & Co., London.]

And C. O. BLAGDEN. Pagan Races of the Malay Peninsula, 1906. 2 vols. ill. [Macmillan & Co., London.]

SONG ONG SIANG. One Hundred Years' History of

the Chinese in Singapore. 1923. ill. [J. Murray, London.]

STIRLING, W. G.   Chinese Shadows.   1914.   ill. [Kelly & Walsh, Ltd., Singapore.]

SWETTENHAM, SIR FRANK.   British Malaya.   1907. photos. ill. [J. Lane, London.]
Malay Sketches.   [J. Lane, London.]
The Real Malay.   [J. Lane, London.]

WALLACE, ALFRED RUSSEL.   The Malay Archipelago,   1869.   2 vols.   ill.   [Macmillan & Co., London.]

WATSON, N.   Prevention of Malaria in the Federated Malay States.   1921.   2d ed.   ill.   [J. Murray, London.]

WILSON, W. A.   Mutiny Musings.   1916.   [Kelly & Walsh, Ltd., Singapore.]

WRIGHT, A. and T. H. REID.   The Malay Peninsula. 1912.   map.   ill.   [T. Fisher Unwin & Co., London.]

WRIGHT, A.   Editor.   Twentieth Century Impressions of British Malaya.   1908.   ill.   maps. [Lloyd's Greater Britain Publ. Co., London.]

WILKINSON, R. J.   A History of the Peninsular Malays with Chapters on Perak and Selangor. 1923.   3d ed.   [Kelly & Walsh, Ltd., Singapore.]
Malay Beliefs.   Leiden, 1906.

WINSTEDT, R. O. British Malaya. 1923. ill. photo. maps. bibl. [Constable, London.]

Malayan Memories. 1916. ill. [Kelly & Walsh, Ltd., Singapore.]

MALAY LANGUAGE

MAXWELL, W. B. Manual of the Malay Language. 1920. [Kegan, Paul, Trench & Trubner, London.]

SHELLABEAR, W. G. English-Malay Dictionary. 1916. [M. P. H., Singapore.]

Malay-English Vocabulary. 1912. [M. P. H., Singapore.]

Practical Malay Grammar. 1921. 4th ed. [M. P. H., Singapore.]

SWETTENHAM, SIR FRANK. English-Malay Vocabulary. 1922. 12th ed. [Kelly & Walsh, Ltd., Singapore.]

WILKINSON, R. J. Malay-English Dictionary. 1903. [Kelly and Walsh, Ltd., Singapore.]

Abridged Malay-English Dictionary, 2d ed. 1919. [F. M. S. Government Press, Kuala Lumpur.]

WINSTEDT, R. O. Colloquial Malay. 1920. 2d ed. [Kelly and Walsh, Ltd., Singapore.]

A Dictionary of Colloquial Malay: Malay-

English and English-Malay. 1920. [Kelly & Walsh, Ltd., Singapore.]

An English-Malay Dictionary. 1922. 2d ed. [Kelly and Walsh, Ltd., Singapore.]

Malay Grammar. 1913. [Clarendon Press, Oxford.]

Kelly & Walsh's Handbook of the Malay Language, for the use of Tourists.

Some other Oxford Paperbacks for readers interested in Central Asia,
China and South-East Asia, past and present

CAMBODIA
GEORGE COEDÈS
Angkor

MALCOLM MacDONALD
Angkor and the Khmers*

CENTRAL ASIA
ANDRÉ GUIBAUT
Tibetan Venture

PETER FLEMING
Bayonets to Lhasa

LADY MACARTNEY
An English Lady in Chinese
Turkestan

DIANA SHIPTON
The Antique Land

C. P. SKRINE AND
PAMELA NIGHTINGALE
Macartney at Kashgar*

ALBERT VON LE COQ
Buried Treasures of Chinese
Turkestan

AITCHEN K. WU
Turkistan Tumult

CHINA
All About Shanghai: A Standard
Guide

HAROLD ACTON
Peonies and Ponies

VICKI BAUM
Shanghai '37

ERNEST BRAMAH
Kai Lung's Golden Hours*

ERNEST BRAMAH
The Wallet of Kai Lung*

ANN BRIDGE
The Ginger Griffin

CHANG HSIN-HAI
The Fabulous Concubine*

CARL CROW
Handbook for China

PETER FLEMING
The Siege at Peking

MARY HOOKER
Behind the Scenes in Peking

CORRINNE LAMB
The Chinese Festive Board

W. SOMERSET
MAUGHAM
On a Chinese Screen*

G. E. MORRISON
An Australian in China

PETER QUENNELL
Superficial Journey through
Tokyo and Peking

OSBERT SITWELL
Escape with Me! An Oriental
Sketch-book

J. A. TURNER
Kwang Tung or Five Years in
South China

HONG KONG AND
MACAU
AUSTIN COATES
City of Broken Promises

AUSTIN COATES
A Macao Narrative

AUSTIN COATES
Myself a Mandarin

AUSTIN COATES
The Road

The Hong Kong Guide 1893

INDONESIA
S. TAKDIR
ALISJAHBANA
Indonesia: Social and Cultural
Revolution

DAVID ATTENBOROUGH
Zoo Quest for a Dragon*

VICKI BAUM
A Tale from Bali*

'BENGAL CIVILIAN'
Rambles in Java and the Straits
in 1852

MIGUEL COVARRUBIAS
Island of Bali*

BERYL DE ZOETE AND
WALTER SPIES
Dance and Drama in Bali

AUGUSTA DE WIT
Java: Facts and Fancies

JACQUES DUMARÇAY
Borobudur

JACQUES DUMARÇAY
The Temples of Java

ANNA FORBES
Unbeaten Tracks in Islands of the
Far East

GEOFFREY GORER
Bali and Angkor

JENNIFER LINDSAY
Javanese Gamelan

EDWIN M. LOEB
Sumatra: Its History and People

MOCHTAR LUBIS
The Outlaw and Other Stories

MOCHTAR LUBIS
Twilight in Djakarta

MADELON H. LULOFS
Coolie*

MADELON H. LULOFS
Rubber

COLIN McPHEE
A House in Bali*

ERIC MJOBERG
Forest Life and Adventures in the
Malay Archipelago

HICKMAN POWELL
The Last Paradise

E. R. SCIDMORE
Java, The Garden of the East

MICHAEL SMITHIES
Yogyakarta: Cultural Heart of
Indonesia

LADISLAO SZÉKELY
Tropic Fever: The Adventures of
a Planter in Sumatra

EDWARD C. VAN NESS
AND SHITA
PRAWIROHARDJO
Javanese Wayang Kulit

MALAYSIA
ISABELLA L. BIRD
The Golden Chersonese: Travels
in Malaya in 1879

MARGARET BROOKE
THE RANEE OF
SARAWAK
My Life in Sarawak

HENRI FAUCONNIER
The Soul of Malaya

W. R. GEDDES
Nine Dayak Nights

A. G. GLENISTER
The Birds of the Malay Peninsula,
Singapore and Penang

C. W. HARRISON
Illustrated Guide to the Federated
Malay States (1923)

BARBARA HARRISSON
Orang-Utan

TOM HARRISSON
World Within: A Borneo Story

CHARLES HOSE
The Field-Book of a Jungle-Wallah

EMILY INNES
The Chersonese with the
Gilding Off

W. SOMERSET
MAUGHAM
Ah King and Other Stories*

W. SOMERSET
MAUGHAM
The Casuarina Tree*

MARY McMINNIES
The Flying Fox*

ROBERT PAYNE
The White Rajahs of Sarawak

OWEN RUTTER
The Pirate Wind

ROBERT W. SHELFORD
A Naturalist in Borneo

CARVETH WELLS
Six Years in the Malay Jungle

SINGAPORE
RUSSELL GRENFELL
Main Fleet to Singapore

R. W. E. HARPER AND
HARRY MILLER
Singapore Mutiny

JANET LIM
Sold for Silver

G. M. REITH
Handbook to Singapore (1907)

C. E. WURTZBURG
Raffles of the Eastern Isles

THAILAND
CARL BOCK
Temples and Elephants

REGINALD CAMPBELL
Teak-Wallah

MALCOLM SMITH
A Physician at the Court of Siam

ERNEST YOUNG
The Kingdom of the Yellow Robe

Titles marked with an asterisk have restricted rights.